NO VACCINE FOR STUPID

by

Camille Nesler

Edited by Vaughanda Bowie

TigerEye Publications
P.O. Box 6382
Springdale, AR 72766
www.TigerEyePubs.com

NO VACCINE FOR STUPID

This is a work of fiction. Names, places, characters and incidents are either the product of the author's imagination, or are used fictitiously. Any resemblance to actual persons, living or dead, events, or locales is entirely coincidental.

ISBN: 978-1475007312

Printed in USA

Acknowledgements

This book would not have been possible without the love and support of my wonderful husband Nick with his awesome editing skills. Thanks so much for coming out of journalism retirement to help me.

I also want to acknowledge my good friend Andrea for all her encouragement and for asking me on a regular basis, "what nonsense got sent your way today?"

To my mother who kept every story I ever wrote as a child, and all my newspaper articles and columns, thank you for always believing in me and encouraging me to "write it all down."

Last but not least I want to give a big thanks to all the staff and students at my school for providing me with hilarious situations on a daily basis. Without you there would be no book.

Dedication

This book is dedicated to school nurses everywhere. I feel your pain.

No Vaccine for Stupid

Chapter 1

Nope, I Don't Love Kids

Someone once said to me, "Wow, to work as a school nurse you must really *love* children." Well, they were wrong: I don't love kids. In fact, I don't even *like* kids that much. A better statement would be that I can *tolerate* children, and even that is only in small doses.

Unfortunately, I didn't come to this conclusion until I was well into my 30's and was already working at a school. The realization finally came to me after a particularly exasperating day at work when I was complaining to my husband Nick about a child who was a frequent visitor to my office.

"He never has a good reason to come see me, he only wants to skip out of class and he irritates the heck out of me by talking non-stop," I said. "In fact, he doesn't even have to open his *mouth* to put me in a bad mood! There's just something about him that reminds me of that annoying kid Ralphie from the movie '*A Christmas Story*' and I cringe every time he walks through the door…isn't that awful?"

"What's so awful about it," Nick wanted to know.

"He's only a child," I said. "I'm supposed to like all children."

"Why do you think that? You don't like all adults, do you?"

"Well no, but that's different," I said.

"Camille, there's nothing different about it," Nick informed me. "Children are just small adults. They've already developed bad habits and unique personalities and some of them you're just not going to like. Besides, you like *some* children, don't you?"

"I like *our* kids," I told him, "I like well-behaved kids…and kids that don't whine all the time."

"You just eliminated more than 90% of the child population," he told me with a laugh. "Anyway, none of them ever *know* you don't like them, do they?"

"Of course not!" I said indignantly. "They think I'm the best nurse in the whole world and they want to hug me all the time! In fact, I need a sign on my office wall that says "NO TOUCHY!"

"Well that's all that matters," he told me, "so quit worrying about it."

The more I thought about it the more I realized he was right and once all that guilt was gone, I felt great. Now when people say to me, "You sure must love children," I just look at them, smile and say, "Well, I do love my *job*." And that's the truth. I've worked in every type of nursing facility from hospitals to nursing homes to doctor offices to mental health wards, and a school setting is definitely head and shoulders above all of those. This job also gives me summers off with my kids and my husband who is an 8th grade science teacher. All that free time gives me plenty of opportunities to write and trust me I get plenty of humorous material each day from the multitude of students who troop through my office.

When I first took the job I assumed I would be conducting the various exams required by the state such as vision and hearing, and treating things such as skinned knees and upset stomachs. That's a logical assumption to make, right? Never in a million years did I think I'd have children sent to me because they had chapped lips or because they needed to blow their nose. And that's just the tip of the iceberg. Believe it or not, I've had kids sent to me with passes from the teachers that read "his nose itches" or "she's sleepy today" and even "he didn't like lunch so he didn't eat today."

It's not just random occurrences either, oh no. I deal with nonsense on a daily basis, and I have the nurse notes to prove it. I get ridiculous notes from teachers all day long that say stuff like, "he chewed too much at lunch" or "foot is asleep," like there is anything in the world I can do for those types of complaints. And through it all there is one thing I just can't understand: Why aren't the adults using their brains? I mean, I expect *children* to invent every excuse under the sun to get out of class, but what is the teacher's excuse? If I had dared to fall asleep in one of my classes it would have earned me a trip to the principal's office, not the school nurse. We're not talking rocket science here. If a kid tells you their nose itches, tell them to scratch it and be done with it. What has happened to good old-fashioned common sense? I'm beginning to think everyone who works in a school setting must eventually lose theirs. I sure hope I'm not next!

Chapter 2

I Ate a Bug…or Something Like It

Ever notice how kids like to stick everything under the sun into their mouth? And it doesn't matter what age they are either. You'd think they would know better the older they get but that hasn't been my experience so far. The kids at my school have swallowed everything from bugs to rocks to parts of a pen, and I'm talking every age from Kindergarten to Jr. High. But what's even more amazing are the responses of the teachers when it happens. You would think after being around kids for years on a daily basis they would know stuff like this is a regular occurrence but I'm actually surprised that none of them have called 911 yet.

Take for example the teacher who came flying into my office with an 8-year old in tow, hollering, "He just swallowed a pebble from the playground and you need to do something about it right now!"

"I didn't swallow it on purpose," the child insisted. "It just flew up into my mouth by accident." Clearly he had his story all straight to tell mom and dad, and the teacher was definitely more shaken by the incident than the student was. "I don't care how it happened," she told me, "I just want you to fix it."

"And exactly what would you suggest I do to 'fix it'," I asked her. "Run a scope down his throat?"

"So you aren't going to do *anything* for him?" she asked, clearly flustered. "Sure I am," I told her. "I'm going to send a note home to his parents telling them to watch his poop for the next few days to make sure it passes out." At this point her face started to turn a little green. "Well isn't that something that *you* should be doing as the nurse?" she demanded to know.

I couldn't believe she was actually serious. "You want me to go *home* with this child for the next 48-hours and make sure he craps out a rock?" I said. "Are you kidding me?"

Clearly she wasn't and sadly, it took our principal to straighten her out on the matter. Hey, I'm not above calling for reinforcements. Especially, when I'm right!

The 15-year old who ate a bug was a different matter all-together. Apparently, this kid had swallowed things before because he was quite familiar with the drill. "I know, I know," he told me with a bored look on his face. "I'm going to have to wait until it passes out."

"Um, until what passes?" I asked. "The fly," he said. "It landed on my sandwich just before I took a bite and it was too late to stop chewing."

"Your teacher sent you to see the nurse because you swallowed a *fly*?" I asked him, flabbergasted. "Just a fly and nothing else? He nodded and handed me the nurse pass that he'd brought from his teacher. It simply read: student ate foreign object. Please advise.

"Had his extra protein for the day," I wrote back. Sometimes, less is more.

Chapter 3

Boys with PMS

I think I need to go back to nursing school, because I'm not familiar with a serious condition known as male PMS. Recently I saw my first case of it. This 14-year old boy came into my office holding his stomach and complaining quite loudly.

"It's just awful," he told me. "I caught it from my sister."

Now I have a strict policy at the school where I work regarding what I will and what I won't send a child home for. When it comes to stomachaches, if the kid isn't throwing up or running a fever, they get to stay at school. Let's face it, we all have minor aches and pains every once in a while and we can't all run home every time it happens. Somehow, we have to get this habit passed on to today's children or we're going to end up with a generation full of slackers who expect their bosses to let them go home every time they stub their toe. Like my mom always said, "Suck it up and go on!" She instilled the kind of work ethic in me that has my happy self at work every day unless I'm barfing up a lung, but somehow, I don't think parents are passing that on anymore.

This particular kid was determined I was going to send him home despite the fact he didn't have any symptoms. "I know I've caught it," he informed me.

"My mom and sister *both* have it and I live in the same house with them."

"Do they have the stomach flu?" I asked him. "Are they throwing up?"

"No it's worse," he said, clutching his stomach. "My dad said they have PMS."

"Let me get this straight," I said, crossing my arms and glaring at him. "You're standing here in front of me trying to convince me you are suffering from PMS?"

"That's what it is," he insisted, starting to look a little unsure of himself. I told him we better call dad right away to give him the bad news. "Hello, Mr. Roberts? This is the nurse at your son's school. I have Michael in my office and he insists that he has PMS. What would you like me to do with him?"

I can't repeat what dad's response was, but the kid could hear the hollering through the phone from all the way across the room. Miraculously, he was instantly cured. Imagine that!

Now don't get me wrong, while this was my first ever "male" case of PMS, I see teenage girls all day long who think they should get to lie down on the couch in my office just because it's that time of the month. Complaints of "I'm bloated" or "I'm cramping" are all I hear on some days. My stock answer is usually, "Really? Me too. Go back to class!"

If they're not complaining about the woes of womanhood then they're asking for Kotex. Sometimes I think the school supplies the entire female population with tampons for the year. "Look ladies, this is going to happen to you for the next 50 years of your life," I tell them. "Learn to keep supplies in your purse." But it never seems to sink in. Finally I got smart and started buying the kind that nobody wants. Turns out cardboard applicators and diaper-size pads aren't appealing to teenage girls and if that's all you offer them, they'll learn to bring their own stuff.

I guess I should also start holding education classes for teachers on the female reproductive system because it's really quite simple, yet none of them seem to get it. No matter what the girls tell you, they do *not* have their period every single day of the month, and there is no reason what-so-ever to send them to the nurse's office every single day of the month for that reason. Tell them to stop whining and get to work. Trust me when I tell you that whining is not a medical diagnosis: A teacher should be able to diagnose *and* treat it in the classroom. Unfortunately I'm still working on getting that bit of knowledge out to all the teachers at my school because they seem to think I'm just joking when I say it. News Flash: I don't joke.

Chapter 4

Am I a Dentist or the Tooth Fairy?

Am I the only adult in the entire world who had their baby teeth pulled out with a pair of needle-nose pliers? Now I know we've all heard of tying the tooth to a string, tying the other end to a doorknob and then slamming the door shut, but surely someone else has heard the pliers story…right? Trust me the experience is still burned into my brain. I made the grievous mistake of telling my mother about my first loose tooth when I was only 7 years old. Did she advise me to wiggle it? Guess again. Did she suggest I eat something hard and crunchy like an apple? Nope. Instead, she took my dad's needle-nose pliers out of the fishing tackle box, wrapped them in gauze and yanked out my tooth. Well, that experience cured me of complaining about loose teeth ever again. I never told her about another one until I'd pulled the thing out myself.

These days most children don't go to the dentist over a loose baby tooth. Losing baby teeth is a natural process that happens to all of us at some point in our childhood. Instead, we advise our children to wiggle on the tooth to loosen it up or we tell them to bite into something hard to make it fall out. Those are simple instructions and it doesn't require a medical degree to give them. So why do all the elementary kids get sent to me every time they have a tooth with the least little bit of "wiggle" to it? The last time I checked, the certificate on my wall said nurse, not dentist. And the last time I checked, there weren't any extraction devices thrown in with my Band-Aids or any Novacaine in with my bags of cough drops. It's a complete waste of time for children to leave class and miss instructional time just to tell the nurse they have a loose tooth.

It's not just the loose ones that get sent my way, either. Every time a tooth actually falls out, they get sent to me, too. The kids present their teeth to me in all kinds of containers from envelopes to plastic baggies to pencil boxes. "Look at this!" They will announce proudly, "I lost it at lunch while I was eating!" They are usually accompanied by a nurse pass that reads "lost a tooth" like there's something I'm supposed to *do* about it. So I guess now I'm the tooth fairy. Are the teachers expecting me to give the kid money for the tooth, or to wave a magic wand and make a new tooth grow in right away? I'm confused because again, I fail to see why our children are missing valuable class time to show the nurse a tooth. Now I could understand it if their mouth was bleeding profusely or if the tooth was knocked out by some sort of injury. But wasting 15 minutes and a perfectly good nurse pass just because nature took its course is beyond me.

Maybe I should make a large sign for my wall that says "dental instruments" with an arrow that points to a case filled with needle-nose pliers, gauze and string. That would scare some kids off at any rate.

Chapter 5

It's a P-I-M-P-L-E!

In addition to my role as a dentist I also need to add the title of dermatologist to the name plate on my door because apparently, that's what half the staff at my school thinks that I am. They *have* to think that because what other reason could they possibly have for sending kids to my office with a note that says "pimple" on it? Did pimples suddenly become contagious? Because if they did then I certainly need to break out my communicable diseases manual and read over it again. Or maybe the teachers think a pimple somehow interferes with the student's ability to learn or to work in the classroom? Yes I am grasping at straws here, but I'm trying to come up with some type of logical reason that would warrant sending a student with a *pimple* to see the school nurse.

I should probably just give up because as my husband frequently points out to me, only around 2% of the population is actually made up of logical thinkers. I'm currently still waiting to meet that 2%.

Anyway, I decided I could at least do something to keep the student's time from being completely wasted (you know, that valuable time they are supposed to be in class *learning*) and so I got a whole bunch of free sample wipes from Clearasil. Now when they come to me I hand them a wipe and tell them to go wash their face in the bathroom. That should make everyone happy, right? Yeah I thought so too, until a student was sent *back* to me with a note that read "still has spot on face." I decided this idiocy required a visit to the classroom to see that teacher in person because clearly, they didn't have a clue.

"It's time for a free lesson from the school nurse" I told her. "That spot you see on Joey? It is a p-i-m-p-l-e. These spots frequently appear during adolescence, especially during puberty. It is a common condition among teenagers and does not require medical treatment. In fact, it doesn't require a visit to the school nurse either. I have no magic cure for acne and I can't *make* the spot go away no matter how many times you send him to see me. Trust me his time is much better spent in your class learning how to diagram sentences."

I hoped that would take care of the problem but of course it didn't. Every year I get the same type of notes and every year I end up writing notes back that say things like, "I'm not the Proactive representative" or "popping zits is not in my job description."

Don't get me wrong, I certainly don't relish resorting to that kind of behavior…ok, maybe sometimes I do, but short of handing someone a note that says "here's your sign" I don't know how else to handle it. And it's not just teachers either. Believe it or not I've actually had parents march their child up to my office first thing in the morning when they're dropping them off to point a pimple out to me and ask "what should we do about *this*" like it's some sort of disease. What is up with that? Have they forgotten their own teenage years?

And you should see the look on their faces when I tell them "it's a pimple. Just let it alone and it will go away." It's almost as if I suggested their precious son or daughter had a disfiguring ailment. Maybe I should just take out stock in Clearasil...or put a big picture of Bill Engvall on my wall with the logo "Here's your Sign" and randomly point to it. Like I said, I'm still waiting to meet that logical 2% of the population. Maybe they're all in the dermatologist's office.

Chapter 6

Abracadabra it's Magic

It may be hard to tell from my stories but I do, on occasion, see students during the course of my day for real honest-to-goodness reasons that legitimately require a visit to the school nurse. It doesn't happen that often though, and after working at this for four years I've decided I have the miracle answer our government is looking for when they ask why students in the United States can't seem to score as high on standardized tests as students in other countries: It's because students in the United States spend too much wasted time out of the classroom and in the school nurse's office. Well, maybe I can't speak for our whole nation of school nurses but I know that's certainly the case where I'm at. Kids these days have learned that whining will get them their way at *home* and so they think whining in the classroom will get them their way as well. The sad fact of the matter is they are right. Kids whine, the teachers get aggravated and they send them out. All it boils down to is good classroom management and knowing how to tell a child to sit down and be quiet and get to work. Learn to say, "You're not dying! The paper cut isn't going to kill you!" Sounds pretty simple, doesn't it?

Now I'm not suggesting that legitimate complaints of stomach aches or headaches should be ignored. Those should always be sent to the nurse who can then perform a quick assessment to determine if it's just minor aches and pains or something that warrants being sent home such as fevers or vomiting. But as long as I live I will never understand why any adult with a grain of sense would send a kid out of the classroom where they are supposed to be learning, to see the school nurse over something like a paper cut or chapped lips. I use those examples a lot because that is the majority of what I see and to this day it never ceases to amaze me.

Another thing that amazes me is everyone's confidence in my ability to be able to magically stop pain. Say for example, a student comes to see me because he fell down at recess and skinned his knee. My normal procedure is to wash the wounded area, apply some antibiotic ointment and put a Band-Aid on it. It usually takes less than 10 minutes, depending on the size of the scratch or scrape. Then I spend another 5 minutes writing up an incident of injury report that describes exactly what happened and what the treatment was. No matter how detailed of an explanation I give, it never fails: Some teacher will *always* send the student back to me, usually within the hour, with a note that reads "scratch still hurts."

Well, duh! I can clean and sanitize and cover up with Band-Aids until the end of time but I have no procedure that magically makes boo-boos quit hurting. As with any injury, it will go away with time and that's just the way things are.

It actually got to be so ridiculous that I had to send out an email to the entire staff that said "sorry folks, but years of nursing school didn't give me special abilities to stop scratches from stinging and scrapes from hurting. They're cleaned and covered and that's all I can do."

Apparently that didn't get the message across because it sill happens on a regular basis. All I do now is write down "abracadabra" on the note the teacher sends to me, because that's what they are expecting. Magic!

Chapter 7

Keeping the Parents Happy? Not!

An elderly nurse at a conference I went to one time told me the best thing I could do at my job would be to keep the parents happy. She had worked in the school system for more years than I have been on the planet so clearly she must have known what she was talking about, right? Either that or all those years around all those children had dulled her senses and she was rendered incapable of speaking up for herself or having an opinion. I tend to believe the latter.

The reason I believe that is because it is absolutely impossible to keep parents happy when you are the school nurse, no matter what you do. For example, if you called every single parent whose child got a scratch or a splinter during the day you would end up with half of them angry at you for bothering them at work for something minor. My policy is pretty simple when it comes to phone calls. If it's something major or something that requires a parent to come pick up their child, they get a phone call from me. If it's just a matter of me putting a Band-Aid on a scratch from the playground, I don't pick up the phone. I'd be on the phone all day if I did and I'd never get any work done. But lo and behold there will always be that one parent who calls me up all indignant, hollering "My baby got a bug bite, scraped knee, paper-cut, runny nose, scratched elbow, leg cramp, stubbed toe and you didn't ***call*** me!"

I always start that conversation out by asking, "Did you get a note from me about what happened?" knowing full well they did.

"Well yes…but you didn't *call* me!" They'll usually complain.

"And what does the note say, exactly?" I prompt them.

"It says that Mikey got a blister on the monkey bars and you put a Band-Aid on it."

"So, what about that injury do you think warrants a call from the nurse? Would you have picked him up from school early because of a blister?"

"Well….no! But…."

At this point I'll usually interrupt and ask them if they read the medical page from the school handbook that details the nursing policy. You know the one. It's in that handbook that every parent gets each year … the one that requires all parents sign and return the last page which states they have read the whole thing and completely understand it. And when they try to say they didn't *see* the policy, I proceed to ask them why I'm holding in my hand a copy of the signed page that says they did indeed read it. That's usually the point I get hung up on.

On the other side of the spectrum are the parents that I *do* have to call. If your kid goes to my school and starts to throw up, or run a fever, or is seriously injured then you are going to get a call from me quick. Most parents are pretty good about getting to my office as quick as they can to pick up their ill child but there are always the ones that ask, "Can't you just dose them up with some Tylenol and send them back to class?"

Well no I can't, you geniuses, because there is a whole class full of other students they can infect when they are contagious.

The next question I usually get is, "Can't they just lie down in your office for the rest of the day until school is over?"

Sorry but that's not an option either. While I don't mind a sick child laying down in my office for a short period of time while they are waiting to be picked up, I am not about to babysit them for the entire day while they should be at *home*. Not only that, but I have a whole multitude of students coming in and out of my office all day long taking medication or getting their injuries bandaged and they don't need to be exposed to a sick child either.

The last thing that happens, and the one that irritates me the most, is when the parents *say* they'll be "right there" and then proceed to show up 4 hours later as school is letting out. How convenient for them. I wonder if they'd come any faster if they knew the nurse was going to call the ambulance and send their vomiting child to the hospital for dehydration, or better yet, report them to DHS for neglect if they didn't come get them? I might have to look into that.

Chapter 8

I Am Not Weight Watchers

Guess what? The government thinks we're all fat and according to the Center for Disease Control, the United States is "continuing the search for an answer" to the growing problem of obesity among the children of today. In fact the state of Arkansas has even gone so far as to initiate statewide mandated BMI measurement programs in the schools. We had a governor at the time of the 84th General Assembly when this ruling was put into place who had lost a whole bunch of weight and wanted the entire state to get on the bandwagon. He somehow neglected to mention the fact that he lost all *his* weight by having gastric bypass surgery. Doesn't seem quite fair, does it? But as a result of that legislative session, I now get to weigh all the students in grades Kindergarten, First, Second, Fourth, Sixth, Eighth and Tenth. Yippee.

Some of the tests I perform at the school are actually good tests and they serve a purpose. The vision and hearing exams for example, are entirely necessary. After all, kids can't learn if they can't see or hear. Even the tests I do to check for Scoliosis make sense because if a child has a problem with their spine, they may not need to be participating in certain sports. That is a perfectly logical reason to do the test. But the BMI screenings? It's a big waste of time and paperwork. Even the experts have admitted that little is known about the outcomes of BMI measurement programs, including the behavior and attitude of kids and their families regarding the results. Well, I can tell you a little bit about their "behavior and attitude" because I'm the one who gets the angry phone calls from parents shouting, "you said my kid was fat!"

Nope, that wasn't me that was the *government.* Blame them. When you look at the big picture the school is actually the one place where a parent can be assured their kid is being fed healthy meals on a regular basis and getting at least 30 minutes of physical exercise each day during gym class. Schools have implemented a whole series of steps designed to keep a student healthy. They've taken out soda machines and replaced them with machines that carry Gatorade or fruit juice. They've quit giving candy as rewards for good grades or good behavior. They've taken all the fried food off the breakfast and lunch menu and replaced it with baked items. They've replaced whole milk with 2% milk. In fact, some schools have even gone as far as to send notes home telling parents only to bring healthy snacks to classroom parties instead of candy and cupcakes. No, it seems pretty clear to me, the obesity problem is not created or encouraged by the school systems. So why then are we being asked to keep track of it when there isn't a thing the school, or the school nurse can do about it?

Let's face it, if the child has a health problem that is contributing to the obesity, chances are the parent already knows about it. It's not like I can check them for diabetes or a thyroid condition and then take them to the doctor for a follow up. Nope, all I can do is weigh the kid. The information I gather then goes into a Web site which generates out a “Dear parent” letter that tells them where their child falls in the grand scheme of things: underweight, healthy weight, overweight or obese.

And what about the child whose weight condition *isn't* related to a health issue but instead a lifestyle issue? Who is the one feeding them all the stuff that is contributing to the problem? More than likely it is the parents…the same parents who will be calling me when they get that letter. I mean yeah, if it's a kid in high school then maybe he is the one who is running to the fast food restaurant on the way home from school every day and the parents have no control over it. But who is cooking for the little ones? Who is paying for the fast food restaurants? Who is buying all the Twinkies and Ding-Dongs at the grocery store? Who is letting them sit around on the couch and watch TV instead of going outside to ride their bike? It's not me, that's for sure. I can't go home with every child who gets an unfavorable letter and make sure they eat right and exercise. I can't demand the parents take them to the doctor for a physical to rule out health problems that cause obesity. So what's the point? The answer is simple: there isn't one.

But at least I may have come up with a solution to keep me from getting those nasty phone calls anyway. BMI tests are usually done in the springtime, so I'll just start waiting until the last day of school to mail the letters out with the results. Maybe over the summer all the parents will eat some Twinkies and forget about it.

Chapter 9

Define the Word Emergency

As a medical professional I sometimes forget the average person doesn't know what I'm talking about if I use words such as "inflammation" instead of "redness" or "emesis" instead of "puking" or "abrasion" instead of "scratch." I also have to constantly remind myself when I'm writing notes back to teachers and parents not to use medical abbreviations such as PO (by mouth) or RRR (regular rate and rhythm) or BID (twice a day) because they're not going to know what I'm talking about. I especially have to be careful about the abbreviation SOB (shortness of breath) because I *sure* don't want a crazy repeat performance from the teacher who came storming into my office and accused me of calling her a bad name!

Working as a school nurse I've now become familiar with terms such as "boo-boo," "tummy-ache," and "owie" instead of the usual medical terms I'm accustomed to. I get it, really I do. I'm dealing with small children and they need small words to describe their injuries, aches and pains. Small children also don't understand the word "emergency" and to them, even a small scratch or a runny nose is an emergency. But what excuse do the teachers have? Last time I checked, the word emergency was in the regular dictionary. It reads: an unexpected and sudden event that must be dealt with urgently or requires immediate medical attention.

Maybe I need to hold a seminar the beginning of every year and explain to staff what an actual emergency is because no one seems to grasp it. Let me explain.

Every year I'm required by the state to do a series of vision and hearing exams on students in addition to BMI screenings and exams for Scoliosis. I also conduct a yearly flu shot clinic so all students have the opportunity to get their vaccination to protect against whatever strain of flu is prevalent to our area. I have to complete all the mandated exams within a certain time frame and get all the information entered into the computer in time for state reports to go out. What I usually try to do is schedule a few classes each day to get their examinations so I'm not tied up for the entire day, or weeks at a time. When I first started working at the school I would send an email out to all staff that said "Doing vision exams today from 9 until noon. Only send emergencies to my office during this time."

Well, that didn't work. I'd still get twenty different kids knocking on my door while I was trying to check a student's eyes, with notes from the teacher saying stuff like "paper-cut, needs Band-Aid" or "stubbed toe."

At first I thought Ok, maybe they're not reading their emails. So I started sending out an email the night before the exams, and another one first thing in the morning, with a read receipt notice attached to it. Surely if they read my email, they wouldn't send a student to see me over a paper cut, right? Surely no one in their right mind would think a paper cut was an emergency, right? Wrong! It didn't seem to matter if I sent *twenty* emails I'd still have kids banging on my locked door while I was doing the examinations, carrying notes from teachers that demanded they see the nurse immediately for things as minor as bug bites or runny noses. Like no one else in the entire building knows how to hand a kid a tissue.

Completely fed up, I started putting big notices on my locked office door that read: vision and hearing exams in process. Only emergencies will be seen. Go back to class! But that didn't help either. The students will just stand outside my door and knock repeatedly until I have to stop what I'm doing, open the door, take the note from them, write "emergencies only at this time" and send them back to class.

That still doesn't make much difference though because half of them will return to me within 5 minutes bearing a note from the teacher stating "the student claims it *is* an emergency!" Like they're supposed to take the kid's word about it? Seriously, who is the adult in control of the classroom here?

This year I made up my mind they were going to get it once and for all. The emails I now send out state:

Vision exams are going on today from 9 until noon. During this time do not send any students to my office unless they have been severely injured, are bleeding profusely, have been knocked unconscious or cannot breathe. If they are puking, call the parents to come get them. All paper cuts, scratches and minor playground injuries can be treated with the Band-

Aids I supplied you with at the beginning of the year. You don't need a medical degree to place a Band-Aid on a boo-boo. In addition, all tummy aches, headaches, chapped lips, stubbed toes, jammed fingers, leg cramps, loose teeth, runny noses, bug bites, itchy spots, hang-nails, coughing spells, scratchy throats, itchy scalps and episodes of sleepiness can wait until I am finished with these STATE MANDATED EXAMS.

I was pretty sure that would cover things and I would worry about apologizing later to the select few who truly *do* understand what constitutes an emergency and were offended by my email implying they were idiots.

But apparently, I wasn't clear enough. Right in the middle of my first examination of the year I had a student come busting through the door with a note that read "stomach is growling." I guess my next email will have to explain how "hungry" isn't a medical diagnosis. I'm pretty sure that's something that every human alive would know, but I guess I'm wrong.

Oh well, it's too bad I don't have a vaccine to cure stupid.

Chapter 10

I Need a Cut and Shave

By the time I'm done adding name plates to my door with all the specialty titles I have inherited over the years there won't be any room left for students to knock. In addition to dermatologist, dentist and magician I also need to add cosmetologist and piercer because lately all the bad hair styles, unwanted tongue piercings and three-day shadows are being sent my way to "fix." I wonder whose bright idea *that* was?

There is a strict dress code policy at the school where I work. Girls aren't allowed to wear piercings of any kind except earrings and they aren't allowed to wear nail polish or "distracting" make-up colors or hair colors. Boys have to keep their hair cut at collar length and no facial hair is allowed at all. I don't have a problem with their rules. What I have a problem with is having students sent to me with notes that read "hair is too long" or "they have green nail-polish on" or "please remove their tongue ring."

You may think I'm kidding but I'm not. I have co-workers who really expect me to have hair clippers, razors, shaving cream, fingernail polish remover and cold cream in my nursing office, along with a set of piercing removal tools.

At first I tried to be helpful. I'd give the boy a rubber-band for his hair if the teacher thought it was too long and I'd give the girls some paper towels and soap to wash their makeup off, but that's about the extent of it. There's just not a whole lot I can do about nail polish, beards and piercings and I flat out refuse to be responsible for those things. I'd send them back to class with a note that read "not my department" but even that didn't get the point across. Now I've taken to writing snarky comments such as "sorry, my cosmetology license has expired" or "the barber is out today" or even "feel free to stick *your* fingers in their mouth if the tongue ring bothers you so much."

The ones that are sent to my office requesting a shave always crack me up because honestly, what do they expect me to do? Break a plate in two and shave the kid myself the way they did in the old west with a piece of pottery? Once I send a note back that says "no barber supplies are kept in the nurse's office" that's usually the end of things, but there's always that one teacher who just won't take no for an answer when it comes to cosmetology issues.

Take for instance the afternoon a teacher brought a high-school student into my office and proceeded to demand that I remove both the tongue *and* the nose ring.

"Sorry, that's not my department," I said, trying to be polite. "If you want them out ask her to take them out herself."

"But she says she *can't* take them out because they were just put in a few weeks ago," the teacher told me, clearly exasperated. "Besides you take care of earrings, so what's the difference?"

"I take care of *infected* earrings by putting some peroxide on them with a Q-tip," I patiently explained. "These piercings are not earrings and they're clearly not infected."

"So you're not going to do it?" she asked, starting to sound irritated.

"That's right," I told her. "Piercing removal is not in my job description." At this point most people would have gotten the picture but not this woman.

"So what exactly are you saying?" she demanded.

"I'll spell it out for you in simple terms," I said, speaking slowly and distinctly the way one speaks when addressing an idiot. "I *am not* sticking my fingers into this child's nose and mouth. Write her up, give her detention or send her to the principal's office for violating the dress code, but *do not* expect me to yank out her tongue and nose ring! Clear enough for you?"

I guess it was because she left my office pretty quick and ended up sending the student to see the principal. I thought that would settle the problem but 20 minutes later the same girl arrived back in my office with a note from a *different* teacher that read, "Student in violation of dress code. Please remove piercings."

Sometimes idiocy just runs rampant around me!

Chapter 11

I'm Running a Spa

I'm pretty sure I've done everything I can do to make my office look completely "medical." I've put up posters on the walls of different body systems, I have vision charts on the door, I've got medical dictionaries and drug hand-books on my bookshelf and I even have a model of the human muscular system on display. Not only that, there is a fairly large blue plaque on my door that clearly spells out the word NURSE. So someone explain to me why the students and teachers seem to think I'm running a spa instead? I'm not kidding either. If I started charging for all the manicures, pedicures and hair emergencies that get sent my way I'd be a millionaire.

I've tried repeatedly to let them all know I don't have nail polish remover in my desk drawers. Or clippers, cuticle cutters, nail files or loofah sponges either but so far it hasn't sunk in. In fact, I even had one teacher who sent a student to me because her fake nails were "growing out" and "bothering her" like there was anything I could do about it except give the kid the business card of the lady who does *my* nails. That must have done the trick because she didn't get sent back to me at any rate.

That's not the only case either. I have a multitude of girls who come into my office on a daily basis to complain about their nails and they all expect me to fix them. My solution is to hand them a pair of surgical gloves and say, "oh, you don't like your nails? Gee, that's too bad. Here are some gloves to cover them up so you don't have to look at them." I've yet to have anyone take me up on the gloves but I keep hoping the sarcasm will eventually get my point across. But I'm not holding my breath.

Then there are the kids who come in wanting a massage. It's usually high-school kids who are carrying around backpacks with 20 different heavy books in them. "My neck is just killing me can't you rub it or something?" Or "I just did 50 sit-ups in gym class and now my back is sore, can you give me some muscle-rub lotion?" I even had one student ask me if I could do "hot stone therapy" for his shoulders which were sore from Karate class the night before. Dream on, kid.

Hair emergencies seem to be a pretty common occurrence too. Students get sent to me wanting everything from bobby-pins to pony-tail holders and no matter how many times I send them back to class with notes that read "nurse office only has medical supplies" it still doesn't stop my steady stream of visitors. One little girl even came to me with a nurse note that read "she doesn't like the braid in her hair." No joke! Now how the heck was I supposed to respond to *that* one? I just told the kid, "We all have bad hair days. It happens." Then I sent her back to class. Short of making a paper-bag mask to wear over her head I really didn't have any other options. Sheesh!

And don't even get me started on feet. In addition to fingernails, hair emergencies and massages I'm also expected to smooth rough skin on heels, trim toenails and, wonder-of-wonders, make shoes magically change into *different* shoes. Or that's what I assume I'm expected to do when a student comes to see me with a note for the nurse that reads, "Student is wearing sandals today."

When that specific incident occurred I wasn't in a particularly good mood so my response back read, "Wow. Really? I'd never have recognized sandals. Thanks for pointing them out to me. Now tell me what medical intervention you'd like me to perform to fix the fact that the child is wearing sandals?"

Needless to say, that child didn't get sent back to my office either. Hey, maybe this sarcasm really *is* paying off!

Chapter 12

I'm Not a Bed and Breakfast

Old people tell stories all the time about how things were when *they* were children. We've all heard stories about how grandma and grandpa walked five miles in the snow to get to school or how mom and dad grew up just fine without their own telephone or a television in their bedroom. I always swore I'd never turn into one of those story-tellers. I lied.

When I was a kid I ate what my mother put on the table in front of me without complaining. I had a specific time I had to be in bed on school nights and when mom said lights out, I knew better than to argue. Apparently that's not the case with kids anymore. If it was then I wouldn't have students sent to my office with notes from their teacher that read "didn't eat breakfast" or "sleepy today."

First of all, why is something like that being sent to the school nurse anyway? Is there a flashing sign on my door that says Bed and Breakfast? Are the words Café painted on my window? I don't think so but maybe I better go check again.

The "sleepy" notes always astound me. It's one thing if the student is laying their head down on their desk because they have a headache but that's never the case in my experience. It usually takes me a whole 2 seconds to find out that they're falling asleep in class because they stayed up all hours talking to friends on their cell phone, or texting, or instant messaging, or chatting on the computer, or browsing on Facebook, or playing the latest game on their PSP or watching the latest episode of Jersey Shore or Deadliest Warrior. I'd like to say that some of them were up late studying or writing a term paper but that just never happens anymore.

I always send the student straight back to class with a note that says "only sick students can rest in the nurse's office." That never makes the teachers very happy but seriously, if a student was falling asleep in *my* class I'd stroll down the aisle every so often and give their desk a good hard kick. That'd jar them awake and maybe they'd learn not to stay up so late anymore. Better yet, try dropping a heavy book on the floor right next to them. The noise will definitely startle them out of a sound sleep and the laughter of their classmates might embarrass them enough to keep them awake. The last thing a teacher should do is send them to the nurse's office to take a nap. Why in the world would you want to reward bad behavior? 20 years ago when I was in high-school if I dared to take a nap in class it would have earned me a trip to the principal's office or an afternoon of cleaning the bathroom stalls. How can things possibly have changed that much?

The whole "I'm hungry, so I can't be in class" excuse doesn't fly with me either. Now it's one thing if we come across a student who isn't eating breakfast or lunch on a regular basis. In those cases there is something the school can do about it such as sending home backpacks filled with supplies from the food bank or signing the child up for free lunches.

But even that isn't a task for the nurse: it's something the counselor or the lunch lady would do. And I have yet to run across a case like that. The scenarios I see go more like this:

Student: I'm hungry.

Me: Did you eat breakfast this morning?

Student: Nope.

Me: Why not?

Student: Mom made eggs and I don't like eggs and the cafeteria was only serving cereal and toast and I only eat Cookie Crisp cereal and toast with the crusts cut off.

Me: Go back to class. You'll live.

Student: But I'm hungry!

Me: And I'm not a restaurant! Learn not to be so picky!

This is usually followed up by me sending an email out to the entire staff announcing yet again that I *am not* running a café out of the nurse's office and not to send hungry students to my office. Hungry is not a medical condition unless you are diabetic.

That usually works for a few weeks until the kids catch on that the whole "hungry" complaint won't get them out of class anymore. Now they tell the teacher "my stomach hurts" to get a nurse pass, then proceed to tell *me* how hungry they are because they didn't eat breakfast because the cafeteria wasn't serving anything sugary or covered in syrup. Amazing how conniving these little urchins can be…but I'm still not sharing my donut with them.

Chapter 13

No Laundromat Services Here

How much common sense does it take to realize it's *not* a good idea to send a child out in the pouring rain to see the school nurse for a runny nose or a cough?

For the longest time my office was in a building not attached to the main school. That meant all students coming to see me had to walk from whatever class they happened to be in at the time. While that wasn't such a big deal for the kids in high school it was quite a distance for the little ones who had to cross the playground and the parking lot to get to my office. To try and make things easier for students, my school set up a "buddy" system to keep elementary children from walking to the nurse's office alone.

In a perfect world, where everyone actually had common sense, that would be a good plan. Or maybe I should say, in a perfect *school* where teachers didn't give in to whining children that would be a good plan. But in my environment? Not such a good idea.

For one thing you end up with a whole multitude of kids who think, "Hey! All I have to do is tell the teacher I need to see the nurse and then me and my buddy can go on a little trip to get out of class!"

I'd suggest they send the student to my office with some kid they didn't like instead of a friend, but then

I'd end up with two kids in a knock-down-drag-out fight before they even made it to see me.

If the whole getting-out-of-class-with-a-buddy thing wasn't bad enough there's always the kids who get sent through a torrential downpour and across a flooding parking lot to come see me for ailments such as coughing spells and the sniffles. What the heck is up with that?

Now I know that most healthy kids aren't going to come down with a cold or the flu just from walking through a little rain. These types of illness are usually viral and not caused from simply getting wet. But what adult in their right mind would send a kid out in the middle of a rainstorm when they already have cold or flu symptoms? Do they really think walking through the rain and then sitting around wet for the rest of the day is going to help the cough or the congestion?

After all these years I'm still amazed every time it happens. Some poor, drenched kid will walk into my office on the rainiest day of the school year and announce, "I need a cough drop."

I'm usually standing there thinking, "Yep, you sure do. And next week you'll probably need antibiotics for pneumonia too."

Then there was the time a teacher sent a student out in the middle of a hail storm to bring me the tooth he'd just lost. His mouth wasn't bleeding and he wasn't even in any pain. The teacher was simply out of envelopes to put the tooth in. Apparently, that couldn't wait until the storm blew over. Lucky for the kid it was pea-sized hail and not the size of golf balls or I'd have been treating a concussion instead of pulling an envelope out of my drawer.

And if that isn't silly enough for you, how about the teacher who sent a student to my office for a change of clothes because he "got wet" when he switched classes? I'm not kidding, she literally sent him across the campus and *through the rain* with a note that read "he needs a dry shirt." Well if he wasn't completely drenched when he started out he sure was by the time he got to me! Luckily, I had a few extra shirts in my office for when kids have accidents or rip clothes but what was this kid supposed to do, sit in the nurse's office for the rest of the day until the rain stopped so he could walk back to class without getting wet? And that's not the worst case either. I've also had teachers send me students who decided it would be great fun to stomp through puddles on the playground…and no one thought it would be a good idea to stop them.

"Her socks are wet and her feet are cold" is what one note read.

"I'm not a laundromat" is what I wrote back. Think that got the message across?

Chapter 14

I Don't Do Drama

I have this absolutely fantastic bright green t-shirt with huge black letters across the front that spells out the words "I don't do drama" and it's my favorite piece of clothing in the whole world. Those words are the motto I live by. I wish I could wear it to work, but unfortunately it doesn't fit in with the dress code. If it did I would wear it every day and point to the words every time some kid ran into my office screaming at the top of their lungs over a scratch or clutching their stomach as if in agony over something as simple as menstrual cramps. I'd also frequently point it out to teachers who send whining children to my office over something as trivial as chapped lips or stubbed toes.

Surely they realize I'm smart enough to know they're just trying to get the kid out of the classroom because they're tired of listening to them carry on, right? In my time any child who whined and complained and carried on in class over something minor like that would get sent to the principal's office for a paddling. Now it earns them a trip to the school nurse. Go figure.

Well, here's a little bit of advice for all the teachers out there who are guilty of this kind of behavior: You'd get a much longer reprieve from the annoying child if you *did* send them to see the principal instead of the nurse. I can't speak for all nurses but it only takes *this* nurse about 2 minutes to figure out what's going on and then I send the whiner right back to you. Whining is not a medical diagnosis and I don't treat it. Maybe I should make up posters for all the classrooms that say that very thing.

Drama and theatrics are just as bad as the whining and I've seen more than my fair share of that, too. Take for example all the kids who were convinced they were getting the swine flu after the school took them on a field trip to a petting zoo. Needless to say, the facility had pot-belly pigs and this was right around the time the swine flu hysteria was sweeping across the nation.

Or what about the time the pregnant gym teacher made the mistake of telling a group of pre-teen girls, "it's just something in the water" when they asked why so many teachers were having babies that year. I think I went through ten boxes of pregnancy tests and saw twenty hysterical 12-year old girls before I figured out what was going on. Hey, they may have just been 12 but these days you never can tell.

Then there was the kid who stomped into my office, threw himself down on the couch and loudly announced, "I just ate a peanut and now I'm going to die!"

I took a look at the note from his teacher which simply read, "Allergic reaction."

"Are you allergic to peanuts?" I asked, not recognizing him as one of my allergy kids.

"I could be," he told me.

"Well your medical chart doesn't say that you are," I said. "Have you ever eaten any peanuts before?"

"Never in my whole life," he said.

I did a quick assessment and still wasn't convinced. The kid wasn't swelling up, he didn't have any sort of rash or hives, he wasn't sick to his stomach and he wasn't wheezing or having any trouble breathing.

"Are you *sure* you've never eaten a peanut before? I asked. "What about peanut butter sandwiches?"

"I have those all the time," he said. "They're my favorite!"

"Well then you're not allergic to peanuts," I assured him. "You can go back to class and don't worry about it.

"I can't go back I'm going to *die*!" he insisted, clutching the pillows on the couch and refusing to leave. "There was a peanut in my bag of trail mix and I *ate* it!"

"Why don't you tell me what grade you're in?" I said, changing the subject and hoping to get his mind on something else.

"I'm in second grade," he informed me.

"And what have you been doing today in second grade?" I asked him. "Are you having fun?"

"We're practicing for the spring concert," he said, starting to calm down a little.

"And what song are you singing?" I pressed on.

"Found a peanut."

Clearly, that teacher is getting the first poster I make.

Chapter 15

I'm Itching All Over

If there's one thing every school nurse dreads its head lice. Just the word alone can make my head start to itch, and that's before I've even checked one single student. Over the past few years I've developed a pretty good plan for dealing with it at the school. First, I immediately call the parents to come pick up the affected child and then I check the heads of every student in that class. I even make sure all items such as pillows, blankets and mats for nap-time get sent home to be washed. Then the school sends out a letter to inform all parents about the outbreak so they can check the heads of everyone in the family just to be safe. It works pretty well, but unfortunately I have yet to figure out a way to stop the hysteria among my teachers whenever we discover the creepy-crawlies.

I swear, you'd think we'd unleashed a mass of the deadly spiders from the movie Arachnophobia the way they act. They start sending ridiculous stuff to my office such as books, pencils and paint brushes with notes that read "Please sanitize! They touched this!" Or, they send students to see me over "itchy spots" in the craziest places. Take for instance the little boy who came in scratching his nose. He handed me a note that read "His nose itches. Check for head lice."

Um, ok. Technically speaking, the nose is part of the head. So I guess I can cut that teacher a little bit of slack. Not much, but a little. Some days I am actually a bit more tolerant of ignorance than I am on other days. It depends on whether or not they made the right kind of coffee in the teacher's lounge and whether or not they saved me a cup of it. But even on my *best* day, this one would irritate the heck out of me. I'm referring to the student who got sent to my office with a request for a "lice check" because he was "scratching."

He came into my office scratching alright. But he wasn't scratching his head.

"Hey buddy, what's going on?" I asked the student.

"I'm *itching*," he said, clutching at the front of his pants.

Well, that earned the teacher a phone call from yours truly while the aforementioned student sat in my waiting room, squirming.

"What exactly do you expect me to do about this?" I asked her.

"Can't you just check him?" she asked. "Isn't it simple enough?"

"Sorry to disappoint you but the school nurse *does not* perform body checks," I informed her. "If you suspect body lice then I will send him home and let his parents check."

"But they'll want to know why *you* couldn't just do it," she said. "And I don't understand why you can't. You're a nurse!"

"It's not that I *can't* do it it's that I *won't* do it," I told her. "This isn't a doctor's office or a medical clinic, it's a school. I'm not about to make a kid strip so we can check him for body lice or jock itch! It's not that difficult to comprehend. Does the word *lawsuit* mean anything to you?"

I'd like to say that's the only time something like this has happened but it's not. The title of nurse seems to automatically make people think you are allowed to perform any type of examination anywhere at any time. I have children sent to me on a daily basis because they slid down the slide too fast and landed on their bottom on the sand. You may think I'm joking but I'm not. I could wall paper my office with all the nurse passes that read "sore rear-end." I'm surprised no one has sent me a child yet for complaining their butt was sore after a paddling, but I'm sure that will happen at some point in my career. I mean, they already send me every single boy who gets kicked in the groin while playing sports. You'd think these masculine coaches would know to tell the kids, "Son there's nothing you can do about it except walk around until it quits hurting." But do they do that? Nope. They send the kid to me. Sorry, but therapeutic massage just isn't going to happen in these cases and the kid *never* wants ice for it because then it looks like he peed his pants.

I'm thinking of sending out an email to all the coaches that simply states, "I don't do balls" but somehow, I don't think that would go over very well with the administration.

Chapter 16

Blinded by the Light

Apparently I now have the ability to make a child go blind by shining my pen light in their eyes. I found this out after checking a student for signs of a concussion after he bumped his head on a tree branch. I knew darn well the kid didn't have a concussion from the pencil sized branch he brushed his forehead against, but in my environment it's all about covering your own backside. Anytime there is any type of injury that involves the head I do a complete check. No dizziness? Check. No nausea? Check. No blurry vision? Check. Then, I shine my little pen light in their eyes to make sure the pupils are both equal and reactive.

In this case, the child was perfectly fine. In fact, he didn't even have a bump or a scratch so I sent him right back to his teacher. That didn't make him very happy because at this point, recess was over and class had started again. He decided it'd be more fun to stay in the nurse's office and play on the couch so he told his teacher he was "blinded" by the light I had used to check his eyes. Most people would recognize this as a ploy designed to get out of class but as you may have figured out by now, I don't work with most people. The teacher sent the student right back to me with a note that read "blinded due to nurse's instrument."

"You messed my eyes up with that light," he told me. "I can't see a thing now."

"Wow. That really is truly amazing seeing as how you found your way to my office all the way from the 3rd grade without seeing," I told him.

"Um, yeah it is," he said, starting to view me a bit warily.

"It really is a shame though," I continued. "The field trip to the zoo is scheduled for tomorrow and they won't be taking any children who can't see."

It's just amazing how fast he was cured and went right back to class. It's also just amazing how I was able to see right through that mess but the teacher couldn't. I guess wonders never cease. Or maybe it's because I'd had more than a little practice with kids who claim to be blind.

I conduct the vision exams at school every year for grades, K, 1, 2, 4, 6 and 8. It always strikes me a little bit funny that the older kids will do everything in their power to convince me they *don't* need lenses, from squinting to claiming they "forgot their glasses" while the little ones always *want* to get them.

"I need sparkly glasses like my friend has," one little girl told me. "I need them really bad because I can't see any of it."

"You can't see any of what?" I asked her, playing it cool.

"You see that chart up there?" she said, motioning to my eye chart. "Well, I can't see any of it at all. I especially can't see the last line."

"Which line is that?" I asked.

"The bottom one," she told me. "The one that has the letters T-O-V-H-M. I can't see any of that."

"Nice try, kid." I told her. "Your vision is even better than 20/20. No glasses for you."

And she's not the first one to try it either. I hate to disappoint them but they're not pulling one over on me. After working for years at a mental health facility, a woman's prison unit, an unscrupulous doctor's office and a small town newspaper, these kids are just amateurs. They don't have any tricks I can't see through with my 20/20 vision.

Chapter 17

I Have a Magic Bathroom

I think it should be a requirement of all parents to tell their children the story of the little boy who cried wolf. Or maybe it should be on the school curriculum for all pre-school and Kindergarten classes. Heck, I'd even settle for physician's offices reading it to all kids when they go in for their required Kindergarten physicals. At any rate, the lesson needs to be taught and reinforced at an early age because there are *way* too many kids making up illnesses and injuries to get out of class these days.

They've tried every excuse in the book with me. I've had kids who claimed they had fevers only to find out they just drank hot chocolate to get a fake thermometer reading. I've even had kids hold food in their mouth from lunch and then spit it out on the floor to try and convince me they threw up. My all-time favorite is when they come limping into my office as if in agony claiming "I just sprained my ankle" not knowing that I just watched from the window as they ran skipping and laughing across the playground to come see me, then magically developed the so-called limp once they set foot in my office.

I've learned from experience that children who are trying to pull the wool over my eyes are cured instantly by offhanded comments such as "I bet a nice big shot would cure you really quick" or "I think

I have some spinach-flavored medicine that will fix you right up, let me look in my cabinet." They're usually out the door and running before I can even turn around.

One of my policies is any student who is vomiting will get sent home. The problem is all the kids know this and while I don't want to call any child a liar to their face; there sure are a lot of "storytellers" out there who try and take advantage of the vomiting policy. Now it's one thing if a teacher, a staff member or another student actually sees them throwing up. That's a pretty cut and dry situation in those cases. But more often what happens is the student will come to me saying "I just threw up in the bathroom." Then I'm stuck between a rock and a hard place. Do I immediately just take their word for it and send them home, or do I make them stay at school? Short of conducting a lie detector test there really isn't any way to tell for sure if they're making it up or not, but I think I've finally found a way around the problem. I call it my magic bathroom.

Attached to my office is a huge stone tile bathroom with a large sink, a huge cabinet and a fancy chrome shower. Inside the shower area is this nice comfortable bench to sit on. Now when a student comes to my office claiming they are throwing up I make them sit inside the nice, quiet shower area on the bench, which is 2 feet from the toilet. The bathroom is 10 feet from my desk and it's not sound proof. If they so much as burp inside that bathroom I'm going to hear them. I also turn off the automatic flusher so they can't flush the commode.

Trust me, if these kids are legitimately sick I'm going to hear them. Not only will I hear them but the secretary, the principal and the guidance counselor are also all going to hear them and I'm sure they *really* appreciate that. Those are the kids I let lie down on my couch with a cold rag on the forehead while they wait on mom or dad to pick them up. But it doesn't happen very often. You'd simply be amazed at how many children are magically cured by sitting in my shower. They can swear up and down they've been throwing up in *their* bathroom, but somehow, the minute they set foot in *mine* not a thing happens. Abracadabra! I should start advertising it as a cure-all and charge admission.

Chapter 18

Excuse You

There is a new epidemic going around and the kids are calling it "throwing up inside my mouth." I can't tell you how many students I see each day who come prancing in my office, perfectly healthy, and announce "I just threw up in my mouth." These kids are usually accompanied by a nurse pass that reads "vomiting." Obviously they haven't figured out yet what burping is, and apparently, neither have the teachers.

The problem is that most of the students know a diagnosis of vomiting is going to get them sent home whereas nobody cares if they just say "I burped." What they *don't* realize yet is that I'm not about to take their word for it. I finally got my new policy in place and any kid who says they threw up gets to spend a half hour sitting on the bench in my bathroom while we wait and see if they're really going to toss their cookies or if they just made the whole thing up. Yeah, they may be good but they're not as good as me. I know all the right questions to ask to get to the bottom of things pretty quick. But they still think they have to at least try, and the latest craze making its way through the ranks is the claim of "throwing up in my mouth." Give me a break!

Take for example the 6th grader who came to my office with that very complaint written on a nurse pass. She thought she was pretty smart. She'd told the teacher she needed to throw up and the teacher told her to go to the bathroom and if she did throw up, not to flush the commode so the nurse could look at it. Yep, I'm all about proof.

Anyway, the kid comes back and tells the teacher, "I can't show it to the nurse because I threw up inside my mouth." Now this is the point where, if I was a teacher, I would tell the kid "great, then you're fine and you can sit back down and get to work." But did that happen? Of course not. Instead she gets sent to me.

"So tell me exactly how someone 'throws up in their mouth'" I said. "You have to explain the whole thing to me because I just don't get it."

"It's hard to explain," the kid told me, trying to vie for time.

"Try me," I insisted.

"Well, it's sort of a combination between gagging and coughing and hiccupping and then there is this bad taste in my mouth," she said, trying to look pitiful.

"Well that certainly clears things up," I told her. "Now I understand completely."

"So are you going to call my mom?" she asked.

"Nope. You're one of the lucky ones. You're not sick at all. In fact, you get to go right back to class," I said, handing her a note for the teacher that read, "Student burped. She'll live."

A few minutes later my phone rang. "I can't believe you just sent her back," the teacher complained. "What am I supposed to tell her?"

"You could always try 'excuse you'" I suggested.

Somehow I don't think she appreciated my helpfulness. But then again, few of them do.

Chapter 19

When the Cat is Away the Mice Will Play

I have a new policy I want to propose at the next school administration meeting: When the teachers have substitutes taking their place in the classroom, I should get a vacation day. I wonder how well *that* idea will be received?

Teachers may not be the best at seeing through some of the ploys kids use to get out of class but trust me, substitute teachers are even worse. Every invisible paper cut and every set of chapped lips gets sent my way when the substitutes take over, and it starts the minute the first bell rings. Obviously the teachers aren't leaving behind instructions for their subs that tell them where the first aid kits are in the classrooms. Or maybe the students are hiding them so they'll have a reason to get out of class. I may just have to look into that.

At any rate, the minute I find out there are substitutes in the building I feel the need to barricade my door. I mean, I can understand them being just a *little* bit overly-cautious in this day and age of sue-happy parents who think their child needs to go see the school nurse for every sniffle and episode of gas. But seriously folks, at some point throughout the day you should begin to use your brains because I don't care who you are or what you do for a living, surely most adults can figure out that a complaint of "my tongue feels funny" or "my nose is cold" is not a reason to send a child out of the classroom to see the school nurse. Right? Or am I being way too optimistic here by assuming that people even *have* brains, let alone *use* them?

The kids are pretty sneaky, too. If one says he has a headache or stomach ache, they *all* claim to have one. I swear, one day alone I saw 20 students from the same class, in rapid succession, all complaining of "tummy-aches." No one was running a fever or throwing up and none of them were doubled over in pain, they just all trooped into my office, one at a time, with a nurse note that read "stomach hurts." It worried me enough to call down to the cafeteria to find out what was served that day just in case we had a case of food poisoning on our hands. Turns out it wasn't a case of Salmonella or Rotavirus. Nope, it was just a case of having an idiot for a substitute who would fall for anything. And I do mean "anything" because later that day, the same person sent a student to see me who swore they were having an "attack" because they were allergic….to the test they were taking.

"Are you having an anxiety attack?" I asked the kid, who didn't appear to be in any distress at all.

"No, I'm just allergic to it," he said.

"Allergic to the TEST?" I asked, certain I must have misunderstood him.

"Yeah, to the paper it's written on," he said. "We found out paper comes from trees and I'm allergic to trees."

"Wow. It's lucky for you there is a whole series of vaccines you can take that will fix you right up," I told him.

"What's a vaccine?" He wanted to know, starting to look a little worried.

"It's a big, fat shot that can cure anything," I said, at which point he tore out of my office like the hounds of hell were nipping at his ankles. Trust me, just the mention of a shot can cure about any ailment.

Too bad there isn't a vaccine that could cure stupid and then I wouldn't have to put up with all this nonsense. With all the medical technology we now have at our disposal, maybe someday it will be a reality. I'm still holding out hope.

Chapter 20

Just a Bunch of Lies

Kids are always amazed at the things they learn when they come into my office. One of the first things they'll do is point at the diagram of the human muscular system that's posted on my wall. "Do we really look like *that* underneath our skin?" they all want to know. Or they'll fiddle with the bones on the plastic skeleton and ask questions like how the bones are all attached or what happens to them when they break. During the vision exams they always want to know how someone can be color blind and it never fails, at least *one* student during the hearing exams will ask me why people can't hear dog whistles.

They expect me to know everything there is to know about all things medical and trust me when I tell you I've been asked everything under the sun from why blood looks blue under the skin and red when it comes out, to where babies come from. The little ones seem to be convinced that I am the highest authority on these types of things and they come up with all kinds of questions.

"If I keep making this face will it really stick this way? Or "If I don't wash behind my ears will potatoes really grow there?" Or "Will I really get bugs in my teeth if I don't brush them before bedtime and after I eat?"

My stock answer usually is, "If mom or dad told you that then it's true." Yeah, I'm guilty of playing it safe. The last thing I need is some parent calling the school and complaining that it's the nurse's fault their kid is crossing his eyes and sticking out his tongue or refusing to wash his face and brush his teeth. Here's a thought: How about people just tell kids the truth instead of making up ridiculous nonsense? It's not that hard. Try saying, "You don't make faces at people because it's disrespectful, you wash behind your ears so your face will be clean and you brush your teeth so they won't rot and fall out. Simple enough for you?"

But who am I kidding? We've been lying to kids for years and making up stories. Just take a look at Santa Claus, the Tooth Fairy and the Easter Bunny. And if that's not enough for you, just take a look at our history books and all the lies the teachers have been teaching kids for generations. Christopher Columbus is a prime example. Doesn't everyone remember being taught in school how "in 1492, Columbus sailed the ocean blue to discover America?" What a load of hogwash that one is. Columbus didn't discover America, he discovered the Bahamas. Personally I'd like to thank him for that because it's a great place to vacation, but why we put aside a day to honor him for discovering America when he never even set foot on these lands is beyond me. I had a great time explaining this to a 6th grader who came to see me for a Band-Aid and then asked why I hadn't decorated my office for Columbus Day like all the teachers had. By the time I was done he was completely fascinated and ran off to get some of his buddies so they could hear the story, too. I'm sure his social studies teacher was thrilled with me on that particular day but I don't really care. Like I said, I believe in telling kids the truth about things and I take every opportunity I can to do just that. For example, the student who came to see me because another kid smacked him in the head with an apple got to hear the *true* story of Isaac Newton, who never once in his entire life really had an apple fall on his head to come up with the law of gravity. But for some reason, kids are still taught that story in school.

They're also still being taught that Benjamin Franklin really did an experiment with a kite in a lightning storm to discover electricity and that is also a big misconception. While Franklin did *propose* the idea, he never actually followed through with it and it's a good thing he didn't because he probably would have been instantly killed. Thank goodness he was smarter than most of the people writing our history books these days!

Chapter 21

A Picture's Worth 1,000 Words

Most people don't realize this but a large part of the school nurse's job is educating the students and staff on all sorts of health related issues. While some of it is normal, every-day practices such as proper hand-washing techniques and how to properly brush your teeth, you would be amazed at some of the things I've had to "educate" about. Take for example the student who had to come see me for daily antibiotic eye drops. The first time I administered them and sent him back to class the teacher almost had a heart attack and called me all in a panic.

"Did you just put Michael's eye drops in?" she asked.

"Yes I did, about 5 minutes ago. Isn't he back in class yet?" I asked.

"Yes he is but you need to check your medicine cabinet quick because I think he took them and *drank* them!" She told me.

"Um….no, he didn't," I said. "They're sitting right here on my desk. Why would you think he drank them?"

"Because he keeps talking about the nasty taste in his mouth and he says it's from his eye drops!" She insisted. "Maybe he squirted them in his mouth while your back was turned!"

After I quit laughing long enough to catch my breath, I told her, "no, that's perfectly normal. Most people can taste eye drops after they've been applied."

That statement was met with a long silence. Finally she said, "You're kidding me, right? How can something get from your *eyes* into your *throat*?"

"It's the same concept as when you cry really hard and your nose runs," I tried to explain, but she still didn't get it. Finally I went into a long, technical, drawn-out explanation about the tiny lacrimal duct in each eye which drains tears from the ductwork into the back of the nose at the top of the throat. I must have gotten the point across eventually or either that I bored her to tears because she finally hung up on me.

I run across the same thing every year when I host the flu shot clinic. There is always that *one* person who insists they "got the flu" one time when they took the shot, so they won't ever take it again. No matter how many times I patiently explain to them that it is *impossible* to get the flu from the vaccine because it is derived from a dead virus and not a live virus, and that they probably were already exposed to the flu *before* they got their shot and it didn't have time to build up immunity in their system, they still insist it "made them sick."

If that was where the whole thing stopped it wouldn't be so bad, but the problem is they always feel the need to *share* their story with all the other employees too, and scare a bunch of them out of getting the vaccine. I guess I need to start telling staff not to come running to my office complaining they're sick if they refuse to get the immunizations I'm offering.

It probably wouldn't work though because most teachers want to override me on medical issues anyway. Kids come to see me all day long for minor aches and pains and as long as they aren't in excruciating pain, vomiting or running a fever, I will usually give them a Tylenol or a Tums and send them back to class. Teachers on the other hand, will immediately call the parent to come pick the whining child up because they don't like dealing with them. Then the parents wonder why their kids act just fine once they got them home and don't act sick at all. Well, here's a news flash for you: It's because they *were not sick!* Let's face it we all have days that we don't feel our very best, but we can't go running home every time it happens. *That* is the lesson we need to be teaching our kids and not "oh, you stubbed your toe? Poor thing, let's call mommy to come get you." Most schools have policies on the number of days kids are allowed to miss, and if they use their days all up on stupid little things, what's going to happen when they are *really* sick or *really* injured and they need those days? Guess they can take that up with the teacher who sent them home against the nurse's advice…or better yet, they can take it up with the truancy officer.

I've also discovered that with students, it's much easier to teach them if you have pictures to show them. I mean yeah, I *could* spend hours demonstrating the proper way to wash hands or brush teeth and explaining why it's so important to do these things correctly but its way more effective when I can pull out my giant book full of gross pictures. Nothing like seeing a huge germ up close to convince kids they need to scrub and brush away those nasty critters. Better yet, show them a picture of what head lice looks like under a microscope and they'll never share hair brushes again.

Too bad the pictures can't discourage *all* types of behavior because I have some great shots of what herpes and gonorrhea looks like, too.

Chapter 22

Breaking in the Newbies

Nothing is quite as exciting as the new school year which brings with it a whole new group of Kindergarten kids, all ready to learn new subjects and experience all the fun and educational things a school has to offer them. Each year we get a whole new group of bright, eager little individuals completely prepared to listen to all the teacher has to say, follow all the school rules and get along fabulously with all the other kids in their classroom.

Yeah, right. A more accurate description would be to say, "Each year brings with it a whole new group of Kindergarten kids who have to be completely trained."

I don't know what pre-schools are teaching kids these days, but kids coming from pre-school into the Kindergarten setting don't seem to be very well prepared, in my opinion. Yes, some of them arrive at school the first day resembling little adults with perfect little hairdos, perfect little outfits and perfect manners. But that's not the *usual* case. Most Kindergarten children these days don't even talk clearly and they whine a lot when they're trying to tell you what's wrong with them, why they're not happy, why they want mommy or grandma and why you should send them home immediately.

Unfortunately, whining makes it really hard to try and figure out what it is they're saying so usually I have to end up guessing. Maybe I should start keeping a big bowl of candy on my desk because candy seems to cure every complaint.

Kindergarten kids also love to tattle on each-other, no matter what the reason is. They insist they are being picked on at recess if someone even looks at them funny, and no matter what happens to them they will always say that so-and-so did "it." Whenever I finally figure out who so-and-so is, or what exactly "it" is I'll be sure and let you know. They're also usually crying while they are tattling and for some reason, crying seems to be a code word for "go see the nurse" no matter what the reason is.

Kindergarten kids also have an unusual fascination with magic markers and sharpie pens. They will write on everything and anything including their own hands, face, arms, legs and clothes. Maybe they're all fans of Mike Tyson or the lady from LA Ink? I don't know but I find it really funny when a teacher sends a kid to me for "writing on themselves." Does it really require a medical degree to send a kid to the bathroom to wash it off? And don't even get me started on glue. My year isn't complete until I've seen at least one kid for eating glue, wearing glue or smearing glue into another kid's hair.

You would also be surprised how many kids going into Kindergarten are not potty trained. Every year I tell the Kindergarten teachers to add "clean change of clothes and undies" to their required supply list but somehow that never gets done. So when the child has a potty "accident" they get sent to the nurse office. *Why* do they get sent to the nurse office? Yeah, I don't have any idea why either. I'm still working on trying to figure out what they'd like me to do about "accidents." Somehow I don't think a Band-Aid or a cough drop is going to take care of it but I can't seem to get that across to anyone. Why they don't just call the parent to bring a clean set of clothes is beyond me.

Another thing Kindergarten kids don't know how to do is button or unbutton their pants before they go potty, and they also don't know how to open a single thing at lunch. They can't open their lunchboxes, their drinks or their Zip-lock sandwich bags. And yes, you guessed it, the kids who have those problems get sent to see ME.

Again, I still don't see how any of this is something that requires a medical degree or a nursing intervention but, if I've said it once I've said it a thousand times: There still isn't a vaccine for stupid. Those scientists need to get busy.

Chapter 23

Because the Nurse Said So

If I had a nickel for every single time a student put words in my mouth I'd be a rich woman by now. I think the most popular phrase of students at my school is "the nurse said so." Usually that wouldn't be a bad thing except for the fact that half the things I have supposedly "said" are well, *wrong!*

You'd be amazed at the things I've apparently told children over the years. Things like, "the school nurse said I didn't have to take this test because my head hurts." Or 'The nurse said I can lay my head down and sleep in class because I don't feel good." And even, "The nurse said I need to drink this Pepsi in class because it'll settle my stomach." I think my favorite excuse was, "The nurse said I *have to* chew this gum or my teeth will fall out!" What's even funnier is when the teachers call my office to double check on the stories. The conversation always starts with, "I'm pretty sure you *didn't* say this but I still have to check." I usually get my notebook out to write down whatever comes next because I know it's going to be a whopper.

Then there are the more blatant stories, usually told by high-school kids trying to leave early for the day. Why they haven't figured out yet that the secretary at the front desk has a direct line to my office is beyond me, but they haven't. Those little manipulators will insist they have a sick pass from me to go home when I haven't seen hide nor hair of them all day long. Maybe they just like taking the gamble that no one is going to follow up on their story. Trust me, it doesn't pay off.

The ridiculous sounding nursing advice always seem to fly around like crazy after a big event such as a flu shot clinic or a school-wide head-check for lice. After a recent outbreak of the nasty critters I spent two entire days checking the head of every single student in school. I also spent a lot of time educating kids on topics such as not sharing hair brushes or hoodies or scarves. But above all that, I wanted them to know it wasn't anything to be embarrassed about and I certainly didn't want them picking on any of the unlucky students who were infested.

"It's not nasty to get head lice," I told them. "Lice like clean hair. They don't like nasty, greasy or dirty hair."

When they looked at me a little skeptically, I asked them this simple question: "If you are staying at a hotel, do you want to stay in the nice, clean, sweet-smelling hotel room or the nasty, dirty hotel room?"

They were all quick to assure me they wanted to stay in the nice hotel room. "Well, lice are the same way," I told them. "They like clean, sweet-smelling hair, not dirty, icky hair. It doesn't mean you are dirty or nasty if you get lice, so don't be giving anyone a hard time over it."

I think I got through to all of them because we didn't have any kids too upset about being diagnosed with lice and no one complained about any teasing, either. Yay, look at me and my bad self! I finally got a point across!

Any child with an infestation gets sent home with instructions for the parents on how to get rid of the bugs, where to buy the products and how to clean items such as bed linens, pillows, stuffed animals and couch cushions. They can also return to school as soon as they are treated, as long as they brought proof, such as the empty box of hair product or a store receipt. I also reinforced the concept of not sharing clothing or any hair accessories. I'm telling you, I was on a roll with this last outbreak, or so I thought.

It seems all my checking and talking and teaching took care of the immediate problem but it sure didn't stop the flow of rumors that spread like wild fire around the school after the head checks were completed. Teachers were calling and emailing me with all kinds of stories.

"Did you say they had to stay out of school for a week if they came down with lice?" or "Did you tell students that wearing flowers in their hair would keep them from getting lice?" And "The kids are telling me you said to use a fruity shampoo to repel lice, will that really work?"

So, that's about how well they listened to all my advice. Next time I'm telling them all to shave their heads.

Chapter 24

Ask First; Then Send

I have the perfect solution to solve the problem of too many kids spending too much time out of class and in the nurse's office. All it involves is asking a few open-ended questions instead of immediately sending the child out of the classroom the second they say, "I need to go see the nurse."

Everyone knows what an open-ended question is, right? It means asking a question that cannot be answered with a simple "yes" or "no" and it doesn't require a medical degree to be able to ask these types of questions. It does, however, require just a little bit of logic, so that may be the problem.

I have kids in my office all the time with nurse passes that simply read "knee hurts" or "elbow hurts" or "ankle hurts."

That would make me think the poor kid just got injured out on the playground or playing some type of sports, right? Well, sometimes that is the case, but rarely. Once the kids found out they could get ice-packs from the nurse, they came up with all kinds of injuries designed to get them sent to my office. The conversation usually goes like this.

Me: "It says here your ankle hurts, right?"

Student: "Yep, it's *really* bothering me."

Me: "When did you hurt it?"

Student: "Uh, what?"

Me: "I said, *when did you hurt it*?!"

Student: "A few weeks ago playing football," (usually mumbled under the breath).

Me: "Do you parents know you hurt it?"

Student: "Yeah"

Me: "And what did they tell you?"

Student: "They said I was fine." (After a long pause and a lot of fidgeting).

Me: "You *are* fine. Go back to class."

They are usually quite irritated by this time but it always amazes me how the limping that was so dramatic when they came *into* my office magically disappears on their way *out* of my office after I ask those few simple questions. And this practice seems to work for all kinds of complaints.

For example, a student will come to my office with a note that reads, "Says they scraped their knee." So I'll take a look only to find a healed scab. Great. That whole trip to the nurse's office could have been avoided by simply asking the kid "when?" Naturally if they say "today at recess" then I need to see them to take care of things. But injuries that are weeks old? I don't think so.

Then there are the kids who come in with notes that just say "fever." Those really crack me up seeing as how I am the *only* one with a thermometer on the whole campus. Kids with those complaints need to be asked the simple question of "why" before they are sent to the nurse. It's easy, see? "*Why* do you think you have a fever?" 9 times out of 10 the answer will be something like, "Because I had one last week," or "I was really sweating after gym class so I must be too hot." If you get a ridiculous answer like that you know it doesn't warrant a trip out of class to see the nurse. That's just plain silliness.

But I have to say, my pick for the most ridiculous reasons of all are when the nurse pass simply reads, "Student said they need to see the nurse." What kind of nonsense is that? Are we supposed to automatically take the word of small children who are notorious for thinking up reasons to get out of class? Would we immediately believe them if they said something like, "The dog ate my homework?" I don't think so. And don't we always ask 50 million questions when a fight or an altercation takes place to get to the bottom of things? We don't just automatically assume everyone is telling the story right, do we?

Not only that, but don't we also always ask 50 million questions when one child tattles on another so we can find out what's really going on?" Of course we do! So why should it be any different if a kid says, "I need to go see the nurse?" Trust me, if teachers would start asking "why, when and how" they could prevent a lot of kids from leaving the classroom during instruction time for stupid reasons.

Try asking, "So, you need the nurse? Why?" You'd be amazed at the reasons you will get. They don't like the lunch mom packed for them. They got their feelings hurt at recess. They don't want to take the science test. They have boogers. They miss their cat…or their dog…or their new video game. They don't want to read. They don't want to take a nap. They had a nightmare…three days ago. They coughed…once. And I could go on and on.

I've tried to ask all teachers to do a little digging before they just randomly send a child to my office but so far it hasn't worked and I've been doing this a *long* time. Maybe I just need to get some detectives and some journalists in here to teach skills on deduction and open-ended questioning, and call it professional development. Everyone always needs that, right?

Chapter 25

There's a Goldfish in My Eye

Through the years working as a school nurse I've dealt with my fair share of foreign objects in eyes. You name it and I've removed it, including everything from pencil lead and sand to loose eye-lashes and those pesky gnats that can fly into the eyes without warning. Still, I have to admit when the kid came flying into my office hollering at the top of her lungs, "there's a goldfish in my eye!" it managed to take me by surprise. Up until then, I thought I'd heard it all. Guess I was wrong.

"Calm down and tell me exactly what happened," I said, trying to pry her little fist off her eye. That wasn't happening as adrenaline had already kicked in giving this second-grader super human strength. The hand wouldn't budge despite all my best efforts.

"There's a goldfish *in my eye*," she informed me again, in-between hiccups and sniffles.

"We're you outside playing?" I asked, thinking maybe a bug had flown into her eye and she was possibly confusing it with…well…a fish. Ok, I was grasping at straws, but second-graders aren't particularly known for being reasonable or even for being very reliable story-tellers.

"No I was at my desk in the classroom," she said, still refusing to remove her fist from her eye.

"We're you sitting by the window?" I asked her, still convinced she was confusing bugs with fish. "Or were you sitting by a fish tank?"

At this point the kid looked up at me like I'd lost my mind. Ah ha, and she'd also moved the hand! Guess my fish tank comment did the trick. At any rate, her little brown eye looked completely normal in spite of being water-logged with tears.

"I was eating my snack," she explained. "And the goldfish dust flew into my eye."

"Goldfish dust? Wait a second…Were you eating goldfish *crackers*?" I asked her.

"That's what I said," she told me, starting to get exasperated. "I was eating them and the dust got in my eye."

"Great, glad we got *that* all cleared up," I said, and proceeded to administer two drops of Visine to the "affected" eye.

Now don't get me wrong, I've gotten some strange-sounding diagnosis from kids before, but usually it doesn't take quite as long to get to the bottom of the story. Like this exchange, for example.

Student: I have a bad train.

Me: A *what*?!

Student: A train…in my forehead, it really hurts.

Me: You mean you have a headache?

Student: No, it's a train, in my head, like my mom gets.

Me: A *migraine*?

Student: Yeah! That's what it is!

Other times, it's not what they think they have that's so ridiculous, it's what they think *caused* it. Like the kid who came in first thing on a Monday morning and announced he had a headache because his mom made him vacuum his room.

Or the little boy who had chicken pox and was convinced he got it from eating the chicken in the school cafeteria.

Or the students who claim they have stomach aches because mom, dad or grandma made them eat their lima beans the night before…or their spinach…or their oatmeal, or anything else involved that they didn't like. Funny how chocolate doughnuts never give them a stomach ache. Or pop-tarts. Or pizza. In all my time at the school I've never had a kid come in and complain about eating something they liked. Hey, maybe I'm on to something here. Maybe I should start keeping a cookie jar in my office and trying this approach:

"So, your stomach hurts because mom packed bologna in your lunch and you had to eat it? Gee, what a shame. And here I was going to give you a cookie, but I guess I can't because the cookie would just make a *real* stomachache worse."

I bet I'd have a bunch of miraculous recoveries pretty quick!

Chapter 26

X-Ray Vision and Problems with Parts

Have you ever noticed how certain professions seem to get taken advantage of? If you're a lawyer, all your friends are going to come to you for legal advice. If you're a mechanic all your friends are going to ask you to "take a look" at their car. And if you're a nurse, everyone is going to think you can dispense medical advice at the drop of a hat. Everyone also wants all these favors and advice for free, too. Isn't that hilarious? I mean after all, if you work at Burger King your buddies don't ask you to cook burgers for them, do they? If you're a gynecologist they don't ask you for free pap smears. So what's the difference?

This happens to me on a daily basis. Occasionally it's the teachers and I don't mind when *they* have a few questions, but most of the time it's the parents of the students at my school, and they don't just want to ask a question, they want me to cure something. What they don't seem to understand is the fact that I'm not a doctor. In fact, I'm not even in a clinic setting here, I'm at a school. I can bandage bloody knees and elbows and I can check for fevers and head lice but that is about the extent of it. You'd be amazed at the parents who will bring their child in first thing in the morning and say, "They hurt their ankle last night playing basketball, can you look at it?"

Well sure, I can look at it all day long, but I don't have an X-ray machine, and I certainly don't have X-ray vision. About the only thing I can do is say, "Yep. Looks swollen to me. How about an ice-pack?"

Then I usually get a dirty look like they expect me to put it in a cast or something. And it never fails one will always ask me, "Well, do you *think* it's sprained? Or broken? Or fractured?" That's the same thing as asking me if I *think* it's going to rain tomorrow. "Well, the conditions look right but without the radar I can't really tell the weather pattern."

Again, without an X-ray machine, my guess is as good as yours. The kid is hurting. The ankle is swollen. Take them to a D-O-C-T-O-R. I know if my kid hurt their ankle at home I wouldn't take them to the school nurse the next day, I'd be taking them to an emergency room!

Then there are the parents who seem to think I'm a pharmacy. They'll bring their child in and tell me something like, "It's burning when she pees" or "his ear is really hurting and we were hoping to avoid a trip to the doctor." I hate to disappoint them but antibiotics are the only thing that will cure an infection and the last time I checked, I wasn't licensed to carry a prescription pad.

So then I get *this* type of response: "Well you're the nurse, can't *you* do something about it?" Yep. I can make an informed suggestion. Take them to a D-O-C-T-O-R!

Parents also seem to think that the school nurse office is a free clinic. I can't tell you how many times kids come in and tell me, "I hurt my knee Friday night at Karate class and mom told me to come see you Monday morning to get an Ace Wrap for it." Or, "I skinned my knee skate-boarding Saturday afternoon and mom said to get some Band-Aids from you on Monday." Here's a little news flash for all parents: Medical supplies kept in every school nurse's office are for injuries that happen *at the school*, not for day-old or week-old injuries that you were perfectly aware of and chose not to go shopping for.

But I have to admit, parents aren't the only ones guilty of thinking the nurse can do anything under the sun. Quite recently I had a 7th grader sent to me with this simple phrase written on his nurse pass: "Problem with boy part."

I mean, how am I supposed to decipher *that* kind of nonsense? So I asked the kid, "Did you get kicked in that area? Hit? Bumped? Did you drop a book in your lap?"

Nope. According to him, he was just sitting in class minding his own business and his "boy part" started "changing" and "bothering" him.

I sent my diagnosis back to that teacher pretty quick. It read, "School nurse cannot cure an erection."

I wonder if I'll get in trouble for writing the word "erection" on a school document? Guess we'll find out soon enough.

Chapter 27

Vomit-phobia

I woke up the other morning and was going about my business getting ready for work when I decided to check the weather report to determine if I'd need an umbrella for the day. I'd no sooner logged on and pulled up the weather website when flashing bright red letters scrolled across the screen spelling out the warning: Imminent Flooding. Go to higher ground immediately. And that was for the entire state! What the heck did they want us to do, go outside and climb up on the roof? I mean I understand the whole boy-scout motto of "be prepared" but that was taking it just a little too far in my opinion. I simply hate it when things are exaggerated. But I don't know why I'm surprised. After all, I run across stuff like that all day long working at a public school, why should the National Weather Service be any different?

I'm not kidding either. It's like the domino effect, or a snowball rolling down a hill. The minute one child comes down with a bug, the entire class claims to have the same thing, and the entire teacher population seems to thinks it's a grand idea to send them all home. And I'm not talking about normal things that would require some preventative measures such as outbreaks of chicken pox or head-lice. No, I'm talking about your ordinary, every-day illnesses.

If little Mikey has a case of bronchitis, every single kid in that class who coughs once immediately gets sent to my office. If little Susie gets sent home for an allergy attack, any student who sniffles once gets sent to my office. And God forbid somebody throws up because that will *really* start the ball rolling.

The other day I had a little Kindergarten kid in my office who was legitimately sick. He was running a pretty high fever and said he felt like he was going to throw up at any minute which he then proceeded to do, all over the bathroom floor. I got him all cleaned up and let him lay down to rest while we waited on mom to come get him. Meanwhile, I called his teacher to let her know he wouldn't be returning to her class. Well, word soon spread like wild fire among the students that somebody got to go home. This in turn caused a multitude of sudden complaints of "tummy aches." There's not much you can do at a time like that except to weed through all the nonsense and find out which ones really have symptoms and which ones just want to go home. If they're not running a fever or throwing up, they get to go back to class. End of story. And trust me, I hear it all.

"But Billy threw up and I sat next to him last week during lunch!" or "I'm sure I'm going to be sick today because Tommy isn't here and he's sick so I'm probably sick too." Once I even heard, "John is my best friend and we *have* to be sick at the same time!" Nice try kids, but this nurse doesn't fall for that kind of garbage. But apparently, some of the teachers do.

Right after I'd called the teacher about the sick kindergarten kid I was sending home for vomiting, she marched right down to my office with another student in tow. “He was playing with the sick one yesterday and now he’s sick too,” she announced. “He has the stomach bug.”

Personally, I don’t believe it’s a good idea to say those types of things in front of children because if they *aren’t* sick, you are going to implant the idea in their head and then they’ll be convinced they’re dying. Don’t believe me? Try it some time. Go up to some small child you know and say something like, “you look a little flushed are you sure you feel ok?” Trust me, they’ll immediately have all kinds of symptoms, every single one of them imagined.

Anyway, I ignored the teacher’s “diagnosis” and proceeded to examine the kid. First, I took his temperature. No fever what-so-ever. Next, I asked him if he’d thrown up any or had any diarrhea. “Nope,” He said. “My tummy just hurts, right by my belly-button.”

Next, I checked his abdomen for rebound tenderness. Nothing was happening there, either. Finally I asked him, “Did you eat any breakfast this morning?”

“Nope.” He announced pitifully. “And now I’m really hungry!”

“Lunch is in an hour,” I said. “You’ll live.” Then I turned to the teacher who had been watching like a hawk the entire time and told her, “You can take him back to class, he’s fine.”

“No, it’s the stomach bug,” she told me again. “The other student has it and they’ve been playing together and I just know he’s coming down with it too.”

"And where, exactly, did you get *your* medical degree?" I asked. "Was it at John Hopkins University? No? Ok, was it at Stanford? Or Yale? Or Duke? No? Oh, you mean you don't *have* a medical degree, correct? Well then, once you *do* get one, you can argue with me. Until then, a child with no fever and no vomiting and no diarrhea who just has a belly ache because he didn't eat breakfast can stay at school!"

"But they were playing together," she insisted, aggravated at me by this point. "I don't want him coming down with it and puking in my classroom, why can't he just stay in the nurse office?"

Ah hah, now we get down to the *real* reason she wanted him to stay with me. I call it "vomit-phobia."

"I don't care if they were attached at the hip," I told her. "Yeah, I'm sure he's been exposed to it, in fact the *whole class* probably has been exposed to it by now, but we can't send the whole class home just because they *might* throw up, and I'm not letting some kid who *is not sick* lay around in my office all day! What's next, wrapping them all in plastic bubble-wrap with helmets and arm-floaties?"

From the look on her face, I'm sure if she could get by with it, that'd be the next step. I swear I'm surrounded by germaphobics. Apparently, all the alcohol gel and Clorox wipes I've passed out aren't enough, or the in-service I had on hand-washing techniques.

Oh well, maybe at the next staff meeting I'll just give in and suggest closing the school down every time we get a case of the stomach flu...or bronchitis…or the sniffles. I'm sure that'll go over *real* well.

Chapter 28

Let's Talk About Poop

Next time the State Board of Education meets to plan out curriculum for elementary and high-school classes, I want to go to that meeting and put in a request. I want a whole section added to all the health classes for every single grade called "Poop: We all do it."

I mean, let's face it, we show that video every year to 5th graders called "Your Changing Body" to prepare them for puberty. We use puppets and other props to teach the little ones how to brush their teeth, blow their nose and wash their hands the right way. We teach about the basic food groups and proper nutrition and we even have the P.E. teachers talk to kids about exercise, and the counselors talk to kids about good and bad "touching."

In fact in some schools, we even teach sex education, provide pictures of nasty-looking STDs and keep a supply of condoms in the nurse office. So why aren't we teaching the kids about poop in the classroom? It'd sure cut down on a lot of visits to the nurse's office, I can tell you that.

You may think I'm exaggerating when I tell you that I see at least twenty students a day complaining of stomach aches, but I'm not. After I make sure they're not running a fever or vomiting, my next question is always, "have you been to the bathroom today?" This will usually get me no response what-so-ever. The kid will literally sit there and stare at me as if I've grown two heads. So I'll try another approach. "How many days has it been since you went number 2?" or "Have you had diarrhea today?" They usually won't answer those questions either. Again, I just get the blank stare. By this point I'm usually somewhat aggravated.

"Look, kid, it's just *you* and *me* in this office. None of your friends are in here, no-one is listening at the door and no teachers are around. *Have you pooped today*?!"

Nine times out of ten I'll finally get a "no" to which I then ask, "Well do you *need* to go?" And when they say "yes" or frantically nod their little head, I simply send them to the bathroom. Wow. It really took some critical medical skills to fix *that* problem, didn't it? How hard is it to ask a student, "Do you need to go potty?" Especially when you take into consideration the fact that every single classroom has a bathroom in the building. Maybe the teachers have an aversion to poop as well?

And it's not just the younger students either. In fact, I think the high-school kids are worse. No matter how much I ask or how many different ways I phrase it, the word "poop" or "bowel movement" is not in their vocabulary.

"My stomach hurts and I want to go home *now*." That's the kind of response I get out of the older kids. Well, sorry to tell them but unless they are throwing up or running a fever along with the stomach ache, I'm not sending them home. But you'd be amazed at the parents who want me to. In fact, one parent even called to tell me at the beginning of the school year that her son was going to come to my office to call home anytime he needed to go to the bathroom. "I don't care at all to come pick him up," she said. "He just doesn't like to go number 2 at school."

"He can go to the principal's office and call home for that reason if he wants to," I told her. "But that is not a medical issue, it won't be an excused medical absence and he won't be tying up the nurse's phone to call home for something that silly."

"But I told him he doesn't have to poop at school if he doesn't want to!" she complained to me. "He doesn't like to go in public and he can't be expected to hold it all day long!"

"Yeah, well, he's going to have to learn to poop in public at some point unless he plans on becoming a recluse and staying home his entire life," I told her. "What better place to start learning than at school?"

I'm not sure she appreciated my advice but it was either that or suggest a colostomy bag for the kid, because it'd be over my dead body that as a medical professional, I'd call a parent to come pick up their child and take them out of instructional class time to go home and use the bathroom.

Sorry, but "Needs to take a dump" is not a medical diagnosis.

Chapter 29

I Wanna Go Home

Someone once asked me what was the number one complaint or the number one sickness I see students for at the school. You may think it's something like stomachaches, headaches, nausea or skinned knees but you'd be guessing wrong. The number one reason I see students is because they want to go home. That's it, plain and simple. Every single complaint whether it is legitimate or not starts off with "I wanna call mom and go home."

Now sometimes that's perfectly understandable, like in cases of, "I want to go home because I just threw up" or "I want to go home because I have a migraine." I know it's hard to believe but every once in a great while, I *do* see kids who are really and truly sick and should be sent home. It just doesn't happen that often.

More often than not, kids will just try the direct approach first.

Student: I want to go home.

Me: Why?

Student: I don't feel good.

Me: Does something hurt, like your head or stomach?

Student: Nope.

Me: Did you get injured on the playground? Or in P.E. class?

Student: Nope.

Me: Ok, well you're not running a fever. Have you been throwing up or having diarrhea?

Student: No, I told you I just don't *feel* good!

Me: Yeah well, I don't feel good either. You'll live. Go back to class.

When that doesn't work, they usually end up back in my office within 15 minutes. This time, they will miraculously know what is wrong with them.

"I do have a stomach-ache after all" they'll say. Or "I think my head really *does* hurt now that I think about it."

"Wow that's great," I'll tell them. "I'm so relieved you're not suffering from some strange illness we can't figure out a cure for. "

"So now I can go home?" They'll ask hopefully.

"Nope," I'll always say. "You still don't have a fever, you're not vomiting, you don't have diarrhea and you don't have a migraine, so you get to stay at school."

"But I told you what's wrong!" Is the next complaint I'll hear.

"Yeah, isn't it awesome? We now know for *sure* you're going to live, because before I was just guessing."

You would think after trying this a time or two, most kids would give up but they don't, they keep trying and trying. They'll whine and carry on in class and the teachers will send them back to my office over and over, when in reality they *should* be sent to the principal's office for disrupting class.

If the teacher finally figures out that I'm not going to send them home, often times *they* will call the parent to come pick the kid up, which irritates the heck out of me. But on a positive note, the little faker is in for a rude surprise when that happens because any student who is sent home claiming to be "sick" when the nurse doesn't authorize it, gets an unexcused absence. Enough of those pile up and they get to spend some time in Saturday school as punishment. Works for me.

Then there are the students who want to go home and they come up with really innovative reasons as to why I should send them. These kids know better than to just say "I want to go home" and not give a reason, but they're not quite crafty enough to come up with a plausible excuse. Trust me, I've heard it all.

"I need to go home because mom has a migraine and someone needs to be there to answer the door if anyone comes over today." That was one of my favorites, right along with "I need to go home because the storms kept me up last night and I didn't get the 8 hours of sleep I'm supposed to get."

I've also heard, "I need to go home because my brother is home sick today and that's not fair" and "I want to go home because Jimmy sat next to me and he has the cooties."

To this day I've yet to send a kid home who was not truly sick and I'm not about to start now, but you would be amazed at the teachers who will do it against my advice, no matter how silly the reason is. Maybe I should try using some of the kid's methods the next time I want a day off. I'll just call my boss right up and say, "Hey, I wanna go home today…because I'm surrounded by idiots." Will that work?

Chapter 30

Abnormal Psychology

I was having a great discussion with the school counselor the other day and I was quite surprised to find out she never gets any sick children sent to *her* office. I'd sure like to know how she pulls that off because I get *troubled* ones sent to mine all the time. How is that fair?

I guess I need to hold some kind of in-service before the school year starts where I do my best Vanna White imitation while dramatically pointing to the letters on my door. "See? They spell the word nurse. N-U-R-S-E. Notice it doesn't say "Psychiatrist" or "Counselor."

Maybe if I made this perfectly clear at the beginning of the year I wouldn't have kids sent to me with nurse passes that read "anger issues" or "test anxiety" or "acts depressed." In fact, the other day they sent me a kid because he decided it'd be great fun to sit in class and bite on his arms. He didn't break the skin so there wasn't anything medical I could do for him, they just wanted him to "talk" to me about it.

"Take him to see the counselor," I told the teacher. "This is her area, not mine."

"Well can't you say *anything* to him about it?" she persisted.

"Sure I can. I'll tell him how stupid it is and how he's not going to get the attention he's looking for and how he knows better. Will that work?"

Needless to say, she took the little vampire to see the counselor instead of letting me near him and it's a good thing. I have enough crazy "medical": stuff to deal with on a daily basis; I don't need the mental stuff too.

Trust me, if I had the letters Ph.D after my name, I'd be more than happy to set up a couch in my office and let them talk to me for hours about all their issues. I'd be more than happy to whip out a prescription pad and write scripts all day long for Ativan and Prozac, and I'd be getting the big bucks to do that kind of work. But that's not my job. There isn't a thing I can do for those types of problems except send them across the hall to see the counselor who will more than likely end up making an outside referral to a psychiatrist anyway.

And if the staff here knew me well enough, they wouldn't want *me* treating those types of things even if I *did* have the proper degree. You see, I have very specific views on many of the diagnosis that are out there these days regarding children and their "behavior." Some of them I think are overused as excuses for bad behavior, such as Attention Deficit Disorder. Others I think are a load of crap. Take ODD (Oppositional Defiant Disorder) for example. It is described by the Diagnostic and Statistical Manual of Mental Disorders as an ongoing pattern of disobedient, hostile and defiant behavior toward authority figures. Symptoms can include throwing temper tantrums, excessively arguing with adults, refusing to follow rules and frequently saying mean and hateful things when upset.

Most experts will tell you this behavior usually doesn't start until around age 8, but can sometimes show up as early as pre-school. Great. So now we actually have a mental health diagnosis for the terrible two's? Or better yet, a mental health diagnosis for the word brat? Because that is exactly what it is, plain and simple.

If you ask me, kids who want to throw temper tantrums and ignore their parents and teachers don't need a pill or a disability check, they need a good paddling. Someone needs to show these kids that kind of behavior is unacceptable and won't be tolerated. Instead, we run around making excuses for it when there *is no* excuse for acting like a fool. Kids are smarter than we give them credit for. They know they're not supposed to argue with adults or throw tantrums or break the rules. And when they do, they should suffer the consequences for it instead of being coddled and fussed over.

Oppositional Defiance Disorder hasn't been around for very many years and I actually read somewhere that it was invented as a diagnosis specifically for children because psychiatrists weren't allowed to diagnosis anyone under the age of 18 as a sociopath. Part of that reason is because a true sociopath is characterized by traits such as shallow emotions, egocentricity, deceptiveness and having little or no empathy or remorse. That describes most teenagers these days! So to fix the issue, a whole new bogus diagnosis was invented and now we have a whole new group of kids on medicine to make them "act right." Silly enough for you?

You may think I'm joking when I say this, but I could find a true mental health diagnosis which actually exists for just about anything you can come up with. Having problems in school? Well, you have Academic Problem Disorder. It even has its own diagnosis code: V62.3. Do you have a troubled marriage? Well then you have Partner Relational Problem, diagnosis code V61.1. Are you having trouble finding a church you like? Then you are afflicted with Religious and Spiritual Condition, diagnosis code V62.89. And I could go on and on.

So you see there is a reason why I went to nursing school and not psychiatry school. I simply don't have the patience to sit around and listen to a bunch of nonsense and then try to act like there is some diagnosis for it, some excuse to explain it away, or a magic cure-all pill. I'm too busy waiting on someone to come up the shot to cure stupid.

Chapter 31

Dieting at School Made Easy

In all the years I have been working in this profession and all the nursing conferences I've been to, I have yet to meet a school nurse who was fat and I've finally figured out why. It's the weight loss plan that no one tells you about and it's called the "I am a school nurse" diet. I'm not kidding either. I've come to the conclusion that children must have some sort of built-in radar when it comes to food. All I have to do to get a child to vomit or bleed in my office is to heat my lunch up in the microwave. It doesn't matter if I want to take my lunch break at 10:45, noon or 3 pm, either. All I have to do is *attempt* to put something into my mouth and they are going to ascend upon me in droves. And let's face it, there's nothing like a few bodily fluids all over the floor and some Ode to Vomit aroma to ruin the appetite, right? Now you see why this diet works so well?

You might be thinking, "Ok, why doesn't she leave for lunch? Doesn't she get a lunch break like everyone else?" Well, I tried that for a while. I'd get in my car and head to the nearest pizza place or barbecue shack to enjoy 30 minutes of interrupted calm, but it never seemed to work out very well. I'd no sooner be in a booth waiting on my order than my cell phone would start to ring. The conversations would usually go something like this:

Some random staff member: "Joey fell on the playground and has a scratched knee!"

Me: "Ok well, rinse it with some peroxide from my office and put a Band Aid on it."

Staff member: "Don't *you* need to come back and do it?"

Me: "Sure. I'll be more than happy to come back in exactly 30 minutes when my lunch is over and clean up the scratch. You can let him sit in my office until I get back. Oh, and make sure you don't leave him in there by himself. *You'll* have to sit with him and wait, too."

Somehow they never liked my response very much, but that's not the only case scenario, either. They also made it a habit of calling me if something major happened, too. Some student could be having a severe asthma attack or could have fallen down and broken a limb and I would be 15 miles away at Pizza Hut or in a nursing conference 45 minutes across town and they would *still* call me. Oh, and did I happen to mention the ambulance service was just a few blocks from the school? Well it was, but that didn't make a difference. Those conversations went more along these lines:

Random staff member: "Billy fell off the monkey bars and broke his arm!"

Me: "Call 911 and call his parents."

Staff member: "But we need *you* here!

Me: "And I'm on my way, but I'm across town and it's going to take some time to get there, so call 911 *now*!"

Staff member: "So you can't do *anything?*"

Me: "Sure. I can tell you *to pick up the phone*, use your index finger and push the numbers 9-1-1! Don't wait on me to get there, do it *now*. Surely I'm not the only person in the entire school who knows how to use the phone?"

So, you can see why I don't like to leave the premises, right? I mean what's the point?

The next thing I decided to do was to make a big sign that read "out to lunch" and hang it on my locked door for 30 minutes every day while I ate. Unfortunately that didn't work very well either because they'd just stand outside my door for 15 minutes and knock furiously while I tried to scarf down my PBJ as quick as possible amid all the banging. Turns out that's not very good for the digestion.

My next step was to make a more detailed, elaborate sign that specifically read, "Out to lunch. DO NOT KNOCK ON DOOR. Go to office for emergencies only."

The only problem with that is children think everything under the sun from a splinter to a paper cut is an emergency, and they'd go straight to the office secretary with every little complaint. In turn she'd have to come into my office to ask questions or get Band Aids, so there was no peaceful meal break in that scenario, either.

So now you know why I'm currently on the "school nurse" diet. And believe me, it works. No matter what kind of tasty leftovers I bring from home or what kind of fast-food my husband picks up for me, it loses all its appeal the second I try to eat and the parade into my office begins. It must have something to do with the microwave and all that radiation it's shooting into the atmosphere. Maybe scientists are right to a certain extent, but instead of causing cancer, the microwave just causes nosebleeds and upset stomachs. That's certainly the case in this place, anyway.

Chapter 32

It Should Be a Law

Sometimes I think I should have gone into the field of law instead of nursing because I have a whole wealth of "suggestions" that would benefit all of mankind if any of them were actually put into place as real, honest-to-goodness laws. Well, maybe not all of mankind, but they sure would benefit me at any rate and hey, that's a start, right?

The first thing I would do is make it illegal for any school kids who went home sick the first week after Christmas break, to play with any of the toys, electronics, gizmos or gadgets they got for Christmas. You'd be amazed at all the visits I get the first day back following the Christmas and New Year's break and it makes no sense at all. Here they've had almost three weeks out of school to play and goof off to their little heart's content, but yet they want to play the "sick" card the very first thing. And they'll use every excuse in the book too, from "I need to go home and feed my new puppy" to "I don't feel good because I'm tired."

Usually, the kid will fail to mention that he or she is "tired" because they stayed up too late playing their new video games, or watching their new movie, or listening to their new MP3 player, but after a few questions, I can usually get to the bottom of things.

Now in a perfect world, any child who got sent home from school wouldn't be allowed to play with any toys or watch any TV, they'd be sent straight to bed to "recover" right? Yeah well trust me, that hardly ever happens and that's why we need a law. All we have to do is convince our resource officers in the schools to go home with every sick kid and confiscate all their new loot. Then after they come back to school they can have it back. After all, any kids who were legitimately sick wouldn't feel like playing when they got home anyway, and this would sure cut down on all the faking episodes that run rampant right after the holidays.

I'd also make it a law that no one could talk about Santa Claus in school either. I mean we can't talk about Jesus, and some schools are even considering taking "under God" out of the pledge of allegiance, so why should Santa be allowed in? I already have enough kids sent to my office for outrageous reasons that aren't medical in any way, shape or form, the last thing I need are more kids coming to my office with nurse notes that simply read "crying." For some reason, everyone seems to automatically think a crying child is sick or injured and they should immediately go see the nurse. Never mind the fact that little children will cry because they're tired, or because their friends aren't playing with them, or because someone called them a poopy-head on the playground. No one ever takes that into consideration at all; they just send them straight to the nurse and trust me these visits always seem to increase right around Christmas time. Some kid will come in crying so hard I can't make heads or tails of what they're saying. After I make sure there aren't any obvious gaping wounds or blood gushing from anywhere, it usually takes a good twenty minutes to calm them down and get to the heart of the problem.

"Sally said Santa Claus isn't real!" one of them will say. Or "Billy said Santa isn't coming to my house because I socked him in the nose!" And another time it was even, "I don't have a chimney! Santa can't get in my house!"

Over the years my stock answer has always been "You'll have to talk to your parents about that. Now stop crying and go back to class." After all, it's not my place to educate children about Santa Claus, and sure as anything, if I told the kids it was all a myth, I'd have a multitude of angry parents calling me up and complaining. Never mind the fact that all I did was to tell their kid the truth. Nope, when it comes to Santa Claus, none of them care. Maybe I should let all those parents come sit in my office for a few days *after* Christmas, when I have another whole group of crying students coming to see me. Only this time, the conversations usually go a little bit different. This time, kids are making statements like, "Santa didn't come to my house at all and I tried really hard to be good. Why did he give stuff to everyone else?" Or "I wrote to Santa and asked him to let me see Mommy again for Christmas so how come it didn't happen?"

Yeah, talk about pulling on your heart strings. Try explaining to a 5-year old in foster care why "Santa" didn't answer her wish to bring her family back together and you may find yourself re-evaluating the whole tradition of telling little kids that Santa Claus really exists.

And while we are on the whole "lying" subject, the last law I would put into place would be to ban celebrating April Fool's Day in schools, too. Think about it. We spend so much time teaching kids how it's not right to tell a lie. We read them stories like Pinocchio, and the Little Boy Who Cried Wolf, but then one day out of the year, we say "Hey! Today you can run around and tell all kinds of lies designed to fool everyone you come in contact with."

And if you work as a school nurse you will find yourself number 1 on the list of people to "fool." The kids seem to think its great fun to run into my office on that accursed day hollering stuff like "Jimmy fell down the stairs, come quick!" Or "Sam's out on the playground and he can't get up and blood is everywhere!" And sure as anything, the first time I didn't follow through on the rouse, it'd end up being a real injury. I've done way more than my share of "running" to a fake injury, just to hear "April Fools" followed by a bunch of giggling. The last time it happened, I told them the next kid to try and "fool" me was going to get a big painful shot right in the hind-end. Well, seeing as how I can't really follow up with that threat, I say we just ban the holiday from the schools completely and anyone who tries to pull an April Fool's prank has to write "I will not tell a lie" 1,000 times.

I've even talked to some of my friends who are more familiar with legislation and politics than I am about my new law suggestions and they just laugh and pat me on the head. I just don't get it. I mean, we have some nutty laws out there. For example, did you know that in the state of Arkansas, there is actually a law on the books which states it is illegal to walk your pet cow down Main Street after 1 pm on Sundays? In Tennessee, there is a written law that states it is illegal to use a lasso to catch a fish, and in Texas, it's illegal to milk another person's cow. Not only that, but in the town of Blythe, California, a person must own at least *two* cows before they are allowed to wear cowboy boots in public.

Wow. A lot of "cow" laws out there. When you look at it that way, my ideas don't seem that bad. Maybe there's hope after all.

Chapter 33

Only the Strong Survive

About two days into the brand new school year, a high-school student walked into my office and wanted to know if he could come up every day to rinse his mouth out in my sink. He had a syringe and some gauze in his hand so my curiosity was just a little peaked.

"Tell me why first," I told him, at which point he proceeded to explain how he had all four of his wisdom teeth pulled the day before and he had to rinse his mouth out with the syringe every day after lunch so food wouldn't get into the empty sockets while they were healing.

I have to admit I was speechless for the first time since I'd started working in a school setting. I see kids all daylong who want to go home because they stubbed their toe, or because they had the sniffles, or because they got bit by an ant. Heck, I even have kids who want to go home just because someone looked at them the wrong way and hurt their feelings, but here was a kid who just had oral *surgery* less than 24 hours ago and he was actually at school! He had every right to be at home taking full advantage of the situation, complete with fluffy pillows, chicken soup and ice-cream with mom catering to his every request, but was he? Nope.

"Did they give you any pain medication?" I asked.

"They did but I'm not taking it," he explained. "I don't want to be sleepy at school so I'm just taking Tylenol every morning when I wake up."

Wow. I was starting to like this kid better and better!

"Ok, well how about I give you another dose of Tylenol after lunch when you come up?" I asked him.

"That would be great, thanks so much," he said. "That'll keep my mouth from getting sore towards the end of the day."

So we had the routine all planned out. He'd come into my office, fill up his little bottle with warm water, draw it out with the syringe and rinse a few times, then pop two Tylenol and go on his merry way. This went on for three days but on the fourth day I began to get a little worried when he didn't show up at his usual time. I was just about to call the front office to see if he'd called in sick that day, when he came strolling into my office with a bright blue cast covering his entire left arm and a big grin on his face.

"You have got to be *kidding* me!" I said. "What in the world have you done now?"

"I had a skateboard accident," he announced proudly. "But I made the jump!"

"When did this happen?" I asked him.

"Yesterday after school," he informed me. "Man it took *forever* at the emergency room. I don't think we got outta there until midnight!"

"And you are actually here today," I marveled. "I can't believe it…I mean I really just *cannot* believe it!

Now about this time, one of my little "frequent flyers" came wandering into my office, holding his pinky finger and trying his best to look as pitiful as possible.

"What's the matter with you this time?" I asked him.

"I jammed my finger at recess playing basketball and I need to go home," he said.

Funny how he managed to get through the entire recess without coming to see me, but the second it was time to go back to class, the finger suddenly seemed more than he could stand. These kids must think I was born yesterday.

"Do you see this kid right here?" I asked him, pointing at the boy with the cast. "He has four gaping holes in his mouth where teeth used to be and a broken arm! Do you see him whining to go home? Nope, you sure don't. If he's here, you can be here. Now go back to class."

Trust me, through the years in this business I've run into plenty of parents and teachers alike who don't agree with the way I handle students and their "sick" claims. Apparently the more popular opinion is to send children home the second they have the least little sniffle or scratch. "Well bless their little hears, they're only children" I'll hear. Or "They shouldn't have to be here if they aren't feeling at the top of their game."

Well, I never cared too much about following the more "popular" trends, anyway. Besides, what kind of future generation are we trying to raise here, a bunch of whiners and complainers? Once these kids get into college, is the professor going to excuse them from class every time they get a paper cut? Nope, he'll just give them a big fat "F."

What about when they get into the work force? Is their boss going to let them take off every time they have an upset tummy? Nope. They'll just end up fired for excessive absences. The earlier they can learn this lesson the better off they'll be in the long run. Or, as my Italian grandmother used to say, "Don't molly-coddle the children!"

Good ole' grandma; She'd be astounded by the things that kids get by with this day and age if she were still around. Both my parents and my grandparents came from an era when kids knew better than to whine, or to complain about little aches or pains, or to backtalk any authority figures. That definitely rubbed off on me as I was growing up and as a result I have one simple motto when it comes to illness that isn't life-threating: You're fine. Suck it up.

Hey, maybe I should have that made into a poster for my office. I could get the kid with the missing teeth and the broken arm to pose for it, too, with a finger pointing and a menacing look on his face like the "Uncle Sam Wants You" posters.

I need to get started on that right away.

Chapter 34

Ferris Bueller Has Nothing On Me

I've often wondered if other school nurses deal with the same kind of nonsense that I do on a daily basis. I've been to several school nurse trainings and conventions over the last few years and I've heard all kinds of stories, but none of them as silly as the stories I have to tell. There'll be nurses at these functions talking about dealing with kids who have feeding tubes, kids who have been severely injured, kids falling over from heat stroke during football practice and once, even a student who went into labor and no-one knew she was pregnant! And it's not that I'm wishing my students would get really sick or suffer from some horrible injury, but honestly, when I start telling stories of kids being sent to me because they're hungry or sleepy or because they stubbed their toe, the other nurses will look at me like I'm nuts.

So, my next move was to search the Internet for some crazy nurse stories. I mean I know I can't be the only nurse on the planet who has students sent to her office for ridiculous reasons. Surely there has to be someone else out there who can empathize with what I'm talking about, right? I pulled up my Google search engine and typed in the words, "silly excuses kids use to go see the school nurse." I figured it'd bring up all kinds of blogs and message boards from other school nurses who find themselves in similar situations.

Nope. You know what the first result that came up was? A blog written by a student, telling other students how to "fake sick" to the school nurse! You heard me right; not only are the sneaky little urchins guilty of it, now they're telling their peers how to do it too! And with the Internet readily available in all schools and most homes these days, they have the ability right at their fingertips to pass on this crazy information, misguided as it might be.

The kid who wrote this blog was one conniving little toad, too. He told children to try methods such as laying their head down on their desk to make their illness more "believable" to the teachers, or to clear their throat several times to make it appear they had a sore throat. He even went as far to suggest they mention to their parents the night *before* that they don't feel good, so mom and dad wouldn't be surprised when they called home the next day claiming to be sick.

Obviously this kid has never dealt with someone like me before, because the things he wrote about would never in a million years convince *this* nurse to call his parents, let alone send him home "sick" for the day. For example, if he tried the whole "faking sleep" routine, I'd simply send him to the principal with a note that read "Little Joey is sleeping in class. I've examined him and he's not sick, obviously he just doesn't want to pay attention."

Any kid who tries sleeping in class deserves a day in detention, in my book. Or maybe a paddling would wake them up?

He also suggested in his blog to, "Tell the nurse you threw up in the bathroom because vomiting will always get you sent home." Sorry kid, but not in my world it won't. If I don't see it, you didn't do it. End of story.

Believe it or not the blog went into quite a bit of detail and the writer even warned kids not to ever try telling the nurse what their diagnosis was. He advised against saying things like, "I have a migraine" or "I have the flu" but instead suggested saying the simple phrase, "I just don't feel good." Well, my standard response to that complaint is always, 'Really? That's too bad. I don't feel good either. Go back to class." Because again, if I've said it once I've said it a thousand times, unless the "I don't feel good" is accompanied by some legitimate symptoms such as a fever, an injury or *real* vomiting, they get to stay right here with the rest of us.

This kid was smart, too. He reminded children to keep acting sick until their parents picked them up and he also told them to go straight to bed when they got home, and wait until their parents went back to work to get up. He also suggested adding little touches to make their "illness" seem more realistic, such as asking for cough drops or popsicles or chicken soup.

These things are all well and good and they *might* work if the kids try and pull them on their parents *before* they leave for school in the morning, but they're certainly not going to work on *me* once they're here.

So, all these Ferris Bueller wannabe's need to just give up and face the facts; nothing short of the pandemic flu is going to get them out of math class.

Chapter 35

Glued Lips? Sounds Like a Plan

Anyone who's ever been around children, worked around children or had children of their own has been guilty at one point or another of uttering the phrase "If you don't be quiet I'm going to glue your mouth shut!" If not that one, you've at least used some variation of it such as "zip your lips" or "shut your mouth" or "pipe down right now!"

In my childhood days if my mother spoke any of those words I knew it was time to immediately get it together and get quiet. And if my Italian grandfather was the one hollering out "silenzioso" in his big booming voice it was already too late and heads were fixing to roll, namely mine and my cousins. After all, grandfather came from a time when children we're "seen" and not "heard" and he took every chance he got to remind us of that.

I also knew better than to run my mouth in the classroom while my teacher was trying to conduct a lesson because that kind of behavior would get any child sent to the principal's office. Or it did twenty years ago anyway. So what's happened in the last two decades? Why have children forgotten what the word "quiet" means? If anyone has the answer I'd sure like to know.

Believe it or not I can sit in my office with my front door open just a few feet from the classrooms and listen to teachers all day long as they tell their students to "hush" or "be quiet" or to "put a bubble in their mouth." Sometimes just to amuse myself I'll start counting how many times they have to repeat it, and once I counted all the way up to fifteen times in less than five minutes. I'm not kidding! I was sitting there debating on whether or not to shut my door and turn up the radio to drown out the noise when a first-grader walked into my office holding a nursing note and pointing frantically at her mouth.

"What's the matter?" I asked calmly.

My question got no reply, just more frantic pointing so I took the nurse note out of her hands and read the following phrase: "Glued her lips shut."

Hmmm. After all the noise and chaos I'd listened to all day long I had to wonder why this teacher was complaining. Personally I thought it was the greatest thing ever. Too bad more students didn't take it upon themselves to try it. But I'm sure the parents wouldn't feel the same way so I figured I better do an examination. I took a good, close-up look at the kid's mouth and even ran the tip of my gloved finger across her lips. There wasn't a speck of glue on them.

"You're *sure* you glued your mouth shut?" I asked her, just to double check.

The kid nodded, batted her eyes at me and gave me a close-lipped little grin. She really thought she was something.

"Did you use a glue stick?" I asked next, thinking maybe she'd mistaken it for a tube of Chapstick.

This question was met a quick negative head-shake.

"Ok then, did you use the white glue from the bottle?" I pressed on, knowing darn well she hadn't.

At this point she nodded "yes" and again pointed at her face.

Now some people might think this kind of behavior was "cute" or "imaginative" or "creative." They'll say things like "kids will be kids" or talk about how "smart" the child is to have come up with something like that.

Well I'm not some people and I have a zero tolerance for stupidity that wastes my time. At this point, I was *done*.

"Open your mouth" I told her, speaking in my best no-nonsense voice.

She just stood there and stared at me, still grinning with her lips tightly pressed together.

"Open your mouth up *now* before I take out my scalpel and SLICE your lips open!"

That announcement did the trick. Her little mouth popped open in horror, her hands flew up to cover her lips and she ran out of my office without looking back. I think it'll be a long time before *that* kid tries to pull one over on me again.

Too bad I can't have that effect on all the schemers out there.

Chapter 36

Common Sense is On the Endangered List

Is it just me or has anyone else noticed that certain traits just aren't present anymore in modern day human beings? Take good work ethics for example. Growing up, the only time I can ever remember my father missing work was the time he had a heart attack and the doctor ordered him to stay home for six weeks. We are talking about a *heart attack* folks, not the sniffles, not an upset stomach, and not a mild little headache. Trust me, after being a part of the workforce for the past twenty-five years I've figured out that nowadays people will use any little excuse to miss a day of work. Most of the time, it boils down to pure laziness.

I wonder what's happened to us? I sure don't think we inherited it because just take a look at our ancestors. Many of our great-grandfathers got up at the crack of dawn and worked on the farm, in the mines, or in the factories until the sun went down, and they worked like that seven days a week. Women were also used to hard labor and didn't have time to be lazy. After all, anyone who had to cook over open fires, wash all the laundry on a scrub board, haul water in buckets for miles from creeks and streams and sew all their clothes by hand didn't really have any other option. So why has our attitude about putting in a good day's work changed so much in the last fifty years? We sure don't have it as hard as they did, and we're still complaining. In fact I can see a huge change even in the last *twenty-five* years, and not just in adults, either. When I was a kid I had chores to do. Yeah, I could play and watch television, but only after the pets were fed, my room was cleaned and the dishes were done. I was also responsible for getting my homework done every day after school in addition to those chores. And the only time I was ever allowed to stay home from school was if I was running a high fever or throwing up all over the place. That was just the way things were around my house, and my friends had it the same way.

Well, it sure isn't like that anymore. Whatever our work ethic has disintegrated into, we are passing it right along to our children. Why else would I see kids all day long who wanted to go home for the least little inconvenience, and parents who were willing to come get them for nonsense? I have three kids of my own and if they are truly sick, I'm going to: 1. Keep them home for the day or 2. Pick them up if the school calls me with a report that they are running a fever or throwing up.

But if anyone *dared* to interrupt my work day to say, "we're calling to let you know your kid has a splinter" or "you need to pick your child up because he stubbed his toe" I'd be at the school alright, but it wouldn't be to pick up my kid and it sure wouldn't be pleasant.

That brings to mind a second thing that has disappeared from our society: Common Sense. If people have it, they sure aren't using it much anymore. I mean yeah, some things I really do understand. I may joke about all the minor complaints that get sent my way, but I do at least know why some of them happen. If a kid says they have a stomach ache, even though it may be due to simply not using the bathroom, in some cases the teacher might not have time to ask any questions so they send them immediately to the nurse. I get it. I am after all, trained and more equipped than they are to get to the bottom of these types of complaints, separate a real medical issue from a fake one, and make an appropriate diagnosis.

But I don't care how long I live or how long I'm in a school setting there are some things I will never "get" no matter how often it happens. Sending students to see me for ignorant stuff, for example. Yeah, I'll never understand that one. Some of the most moronic reasons have been "says their nose is cold" or "has the hiccups" and once I even got "has a sore tongue from talking too much." Seriously! Sometimes I just want to go into the classrooms and holler "*why* would you *ever* think this was a nursing issue?" at the top of my lungs. Trust me I'm making a list of all the goofiness I've experienced and someday, just before I get ready to retire, I'm going to announce it all over the school's loudspeaker.

At least that'll give them some ammunition for the commitment hearing that's sure to follow.

Chapter 37

Hallelujah, It's a Miracle!

I've worked at a variety of different places over the last twenty years during my nursing career and I've seen some things you wouldn't believe. I've worked in almost every setting imaginable too, from a woman's prison to a mental health facility to an emergency room. If you're thinking that type of experience isn't all that necessary to be a school nurse you are sadly mistaken.

My mental health training helps me handle all the crazy mess that gets thrown my way on a daily basis and my ER experience helps me to separate and triage the true emergencies from the "I just wanna go home today" nonsense. Not only that, but if I can deal with a bunch of female inmates bent on staying in the infirmary instead of going to work duty, I can *definitely* handle any student who wants to try and pull one over on me. In fact sometimes, I think the prison was the *best* preparation for this gig.

Take for instance the kids who want to fake injuries hoping I'll just send them home. That kind of nonsense doesn't fly well with me at all, especially after taking care of children in the ER who were truly injured, or taking care of a student who fell off the monkey bars and had bones sticking out of their arms. If you've ever dealt with those types of situations then you can understand the contempt I have for the ones who want to cry wolf.

I used to have a window in my office so I would stand at the window and watch the kids play during recess. I can't tell you how many times some kid would be jumping rope or playing hop-scotch and they'd decide their foot was "broken." I'd personally watch them *run* to tell the teacher then *run* across the playground to my office, only to start limping and crying the minute they walked through the door. That's when the whole prison nurse persona came in handy.

"I broke it and I need to go home," would be the first words out of the kid's mouth.

"Wow. That's pretty incredible considering I just watched you run across the playground," would be my response. "Are you *sure* it's broke?"

At this point I'd get a lot of rapid head nodding and more tears.

"Gee, that's too bad," I would tell them. "Because since you ran on a broken foot I'm sure it's all messed up now and the doctor will have to cut it off." You'd be amazed at how quick they would recover.

"It's really not broke," they would assure me. 'See? I can walk on it just fine."

"Hallelujah, it's a miracle! Now get back to recess and don't ever make up stories like that again or sometime you'll *really* be hurt and no one will believe you."

Then there are the high school kids who can't use recess as an excuse for getting hurt. As a result these students have to be really creative, like "fainting goat" creative. If you've never heard of a fainting goat, it's a breed of domestic goat whose muscles freeze for approximately ten seconds when the goat is startled, resulting in the animal falling over on its side. I've had a couple of kids try this method to get out of class, too.

There's nothing like getting a phone call from a panicked teacher hollering "Suzy just fainted in the middle of class" only to run into the classroom with your emergency first aid kit to find "Suzy" sitting on the floor grinning and saying "Yep, I just fell over."

"And I'm the Prime Minister of Japan" I said. "Get up, sit back at your desk, and quit messing around. Sometime you might pass out for real and nobody will believe it, they'll just leave you lying on the floor."

I've always issued the same type of warning every time I get that kind of behavior, but I'm not sure how much good it does. It's been my experience that the same kids who try to fake injuries are also the ones who make up illnesses, tattle on their friends for imagined infractions and also tell the teacher the dog ate their homework. I'm sure they're all going to be politicians when they grow up.

Chapter 38

Never Ceases to Amaze Me

If I've said it once I've said it a million times, this job has me doing things I never dreamed would be required when I took a position as a school nurse. I mean sure, I expected to deal with illness and injuries all day long but I sure didn't expect to deal with so many gullible teachers, psychotic parents and scheming little children. It sure has kept me on my toes and I can definitely say one thing without hesitation: I've never been bored.

Believe it or not, my written job description really does have the word "nurse" in it. There really is a sign on my door that spells out the word N-U-R-S-E in big white letters, but when I think of all the duties I perform on a daily basis it has nothing to do with real nursing. Instead, it reminds me more of the phrase my mother used whenever she would describe her life as a stay at home mom. She said, "It's a combination nurse, teacher, cook, dish-washer, disciplinarian and every other profession under the sun." Yep, that about sums it up.

Oh well, I guess it's a good thing I have a sense of humor or I'd have hit the door running a long time ago.

I guess that's why employers tend to put "other duties as assigned" on most written job descriptions.

Go ahead and check yours, I promise you it's there, hidden in the tiny, illegible print all the way at the bottom. That way, when they ask you to do something completely ridiculous, they feel like they're justified. Smart move, isn't it? Well, I have a few smart moves of my own. For example, I'm governed by the State Board of Nursing which protects my professional license. That in itself allows me to use the greatest word in the English language: NO.

So you see, they can *ask* all day long until the cows come home, but there are some things I know beyond a shadow of a doubt I'm not allowed to do, no matter who wants me to do it, and I have laws that back me up. Those laws sure can come in handy when you have an angry parent on the phone, screaming at you to give their kid some Tylenol even though you don't have a signed medical consent, or a goofy teacher who expects you to strip a kid down and examine them for body lice, even though you're not in a clinical setting and the parents aren't present. Yeah, after a few years in this business I've found it's much easier to quote a few state laws than it is to try and reason with, well, stupid people.

But believe it or not, it's not always the stupid things that amaze me about this job. Sometimes just a regular, ordinary occurrence can shock the heck out of me. For example, twenty years ago when I got my nursing license I never in a million years thought I'd be doing research on how to treat a scorpion sting. I mean let's be realistic here we live in ARKANSAS, not the Sahara Desert. Scorpion stings weren't covered at all during my first aid training in nursing school.

So what was I doing looking up treatment for *that* particular kind of affliction? Well, after finding three of the nasty critters in our brand new building, I decided it might be a good idea to be prepared. The first thing I did was tell our maintenance guy to call up the pest control guys. "Make sure you tell them it's for scorpions so they can bring out the heavy-duty poison," I told him. "From everything I've found online, the regular stuff they spray won't phase these things at all."

Naturally, the pest control guy didn't believe us, either. "You have a *what?*" he asked with a snicker in his voice. Luckily our science teacher had managed to trap one of the horrid things in a plastic Tupperware bowl, and Mr. Orkin Man wasn't quite as smug when faced with a live specimen.

At any rate, the whole episode got to me thinking about the possibility that one of our students could get stung. After all, kids like digging in the dirt and kids like bugs. It'd be just my luck one of them would think it was "cute" and they'd try to pick it up. Trust me that is one phone call I *do not* want to make. Can't you just hear the conversation now?"

"Mrs. Smith I need you to come to the school immediately. We just called 911 because your son was stung by a scorpion."

Then I'd have to deal with all the hysterics that would be sure to follow. No thank you. I'd rather be informed from the get-go and know ahead of time how to treat something like that. Luckily, all my reading paid off and I've since discovered the only kind of scorpions that live in Arkansas are the relatively harmless ones. A sting might still hurt a little and some kids who are prone to allergies might have a few more symptoms than others, but it wouldn't be life-threatening and no ambulances would be necessary. Thank goodness. Now let's just hope all the snakes stay away, too. I don't have a supply of anti-venom and somehow, I don't think slicing into the bite with a knife and sucking out the poison is in my scope of practice.

At any rate, between the expected, the unexpected and the plain ole' moronic, my job is never dull. In fact, sometimes I wonder what I'd ever do if people stopped surprising me. I guess someday it'll eventually happen. I mean, I'm sure one of these days I'll quit expecting people to use a little bit of logic when dealing with children. And maybe after a few decades in this business I'll also quit expecting the grown-ups to be smarter than the kids they're dealing with. Maybe after years and years I'll no longer expect teachers to see through the ploys of small children trying to pull one over on them to get out of class. And maybe once I'm senile and suffering from dementia I'll believe it's perfectly acceptable to send children to the nurse every five minutes for burping, sniffles and farting episodes.

But hey, when and if that *does* finally happen, there won't be anything left to write about!